SHAM PEER REVIEW

THE POWER of IMMUNITY
and
THE ABUSE of TRUST

Gregory R. PichÉ

DISCLAIMER

No part of this publication may be reproduced, stored in a retrieval system, or transmitted in any form or by any other means, electronic, mechanical, photocopying, recording, scanning or otherwise without the express written permission of the author.

LIMIT OF LIABILITY/ DISCLAIMER OF WARRANTY:

THE INFORMATION IN THIS BOOK IS MEANT AS A GENERAL RESOURCE BOOK. THE AUTHOR MAKES NO REPRESENTATIONS OR WARRANTIES WITH RESPECT TO THE ACCURACY OR COMPLETENESS OF THE CONTENTS OF THE WORK AND SPECIFICALLY DISCLAIMS ALL WARRANTIES OF FITNESS FOR A PARTICULAR PURPOSE. THE ADVICE AND STRATEGIES CONTAINED THEREIN MAY NOT BE SUITABLE FOR EVERY SITUATION. THE WORK IS SOLD WITH THE UNDERSTANDING THAT THE AUTHOR IS NOT PROVIDING ANY LEGAL, ACCOUNTING, OR OTHER PROFESSIONAL SERVICES. IF LEGAL, ACCOUNTING, OR OTHER EXPERT ASSISTANCE IS REQUIRED, THE SERVICES OF COMPETENT PROFESSIONALS SHOULD BE SOUGHT.

TO TAMARA VINCELETTE,

*MY BEST FRIEND, FAVORITE LAWYER
AND BELOVED WIFE.*

A behind-the-scenes look at the sinister intrigue of medical politics. Piche' tells how policing by peers can lead to false accusations by colleagues who are more interested in character assassination than improving the standard of care. Piche' presents cases that show how immunity for reviewers has led to abuse. He offers remedies that could reduce malicious attacks on physicians while protecting the public's right to high quality care. It's a great read.

Curt R. Freed, MD, University of Colorado
School of Medicine

(The) book is a great primer for this area. Very helpful in helping me get up to speed quickly on the issues.

Robert N. Nicholson, Esq.,
Nicholson & Eastin, LLP

Landmark cases, good doctors, bad doctors... shams and scoundrels. A great overview of the circus-like atmosphere that is the Medical Peer Review process. I highly recommend this book.

Errol L. Biggs, Ph.D.,FACHE, Director –
Graduate Programs in Health Administration,
Director - Center for Health Administration,
University of Colorado, Denver

TABLE OF CONTENTS

INTRODUCTION

What is Medical Peer Review?

Medical Peer Review is the process of evaluating individual professional performance by qualified peers as part of a system to maintain standards and improve performance within the profession.

If misused, Peer Review can be a powerful weapon to constrain competitors, to eviscerate political rivals and to energize personal egos through the diminishment of other professionals.

In medicine, under the shelter of near absolute immunity provided by the HealthCare Quality Improvement Act of 1980 ("HCQIA") and state Peer Review counterparts, the system of review and accountability as enacted by the legislatures and reviewed by the courts assumes a high level of good faith and fair treatment of their colleagues by professionals.

Like any system with a concentration of unaccountable power to destroy the professional reputation and livelihood of one's colleagues, there are bound to be abuses.

This is not to suggest that all Peer Review is corrupt or that all professional concerns raised through the Peer Review process are misplaced. All professionals, being human beings, make mistakes. No physician can be on the top of his or her game every day.

All professionals need to step back on occasion and evaluate their performance to consider the possibility that they have perhaps made a mistake or might have approached a problem more skillfully. A major problem with Peer Review is that there is often a "gotcha" element that tends to elevate the reviewers and diminish the reviewed.

There are very few, if any, professionals who could withstand a comprehensive review of performance without someone raising an issue of whether the service might have been enhanced through a different procedure or approach.

One of the ironies of the Peer Review system is that it is not unusual for members of a Peer Review panel to sit in judgment of colleagues on issues in which the reviewers have a far worse record of performance than those reviewed.

Yet, a physician in Peer Review is constrained from raising that irony in defense under the retort that it is the performance of the reviewed physician, not the reviewers that is at issue.

If we were dealing with clear lines of performance obligations that would be one thing, but more often than not, Peer Review deals with subtle issues over which there is little or no consensus and over which any professional could be called to task, if someone chose to do so.

Unfortunately, much of the focus in the Peer Review process seems to be on sanctions against a particular physician rather than encouraging improvement or additional medical or clinical education.

Because of the structure of the Peer Review process, affected physicians tend to view the process as adversarial from the start, which in fact it usually is, rather than a collaborative effort to raise the standard of care for all.

Assuming that there are none among us who from time to time could not use the benefit of additional education, training and insight, the system does not provide for a collaborative resolution that might yield improved performance without the ongoing headaches of legal confrontation.

The HCQIA reporting requirements to the National Practitioner Data Bank for physicians, whose insurance companies settle malpractice cases or whose hospitals undertake adverse actions with respect to their medical staff privileges, creates a "quasi-criminal" system in which physicians thus affected are forever thereafter deemed to have "a record".

The process itself tends to polarize the participants, drain valuable resources and unnecessarily destroy careers. A different approach, based on principles of education and performance enhancement that renders a "quasi-criminal" approach as the last step rather than the first, would be far more effective and fair.

CHAPTER 1

Sham Peer Review:
Power Aphrodisiac

Henry Kissinger famously stated during the Nixon years that "Power is the greatest aphrodisiac." More than a century earlier Abraham Lincoln noted, "Nearly all men can stand adversity, but if you want to test a man's character, give him power."

Every hospital as an institution has a power structure among its medical staff. Powerful members of a medical staff are never the subject of Sham Peer Review and rarely the subject of any kind of meaningful Peer Review.

Armed with control over the Peer Review process, statutory immunity and other protections, medical staff leaders wield an immense amount of personal power over those on the medical staff that they view as threats, competitors, or of a lesser station, especially those who need to be put in place because of racial or sexual bias or just because they get a level of "glee" out of the use of power to "kick down."

> *A huge body of research - hundreds of studies - shows that when people are put in positions of power, they start talking more, taking what they want for themselves, ignoring what other people say or want, ignoring how less powerful*

people react to their behavior, acting more rudely, and generally treating any situation or person as a means for satisfying their own needs - and that being put in a position of power that they are all acting as jerks.

Sutton, *The No Asshole Rule: Building a Civilized Work Force and Surviving One That Isn't.*[1]

The studies tend to show that power leads to objectification of subordinates and colleagues, making the powerful "prone to self-interested, impulsive behavior, be it inappropriate consumption of public goods or aggression." Guinote & Vescio, *The Social Psychology of Power,* The Guilford Press. (2010) at 196. "The experience of power short-circuits the very tendencies toward effective social engagement that group members seek in their leaders - a paradox of power. " Id.

In hospital settings, power historically has been focused and relayed between on big admitters, in hospital-based physicians, and in long time officers of the medical staff who pass critical roles as Chief of Staff or members of the Medical Executive Committee back and forth between a favored few.

Those who are typically victims of the inappropriate exercise of institutional power tend to be new members of the medical staff, women, minorities and foreign-born physicians who do not assimilate as

---

[1] Hatchett Book Group. (2007) (Kindle location 905-907)

easily into the social structure and organization of the hospital institution.

For example, a hospital in Texas had a shelf in the medical staff office jokingly referred to by most of the medical staff as the "Sand Bunny" shelf referring to doctors from India, Pakistan and the Middle East, for ease of access during Peer Review proceedings.

It will come as no surprise that some male doctors are sexist and resent the intrusion of women into what used to be a male-dominated profession. Some doctors also harbor economic resentments because female physicians tend to be more attractive to female patients, and foreign born or minority doctors are looked upon as inferior while competing for patients in their turf.

Loners and those who tend to keep to themselves and eschew the playing of institutional politics are the most at risk.

Although ideally every physician should be reviewed fairly and on his/her own merits during the Peer Review process, the system puts so much power in the hands of a few to "bank" (report to the National Practitioner Data Bank (NPDB) a physician and drastically affect his or her career, fairness and "laissez fairness" cannot be assumed.

All physicians on a medical staff need to pay attention to the politics of the institution for pure self-protection

8

and should build alliances with important physicians who can help provide a level of protection and shelter from those with power who are inclined to use it simply because they can.

Hospital administrators will generally accede to the power structure on the medical staff either out of fear of disruption or by manipulation of those institutionally powerful doctors that they are dependent upon to keep the institution afloat.

Some hospital administrators and physician leaders make it their business to create collaborative interactions in their hospitals, but they are rare. Many are unable to lift the standing of others without feeling diminished themselves.

If the medical staff "Dons" begin picking on you and you have no allies and mentors, consider moving on before they commence the Peer Review process and render you unable to leave because the mere fact of your leaving while under investigation is itself reportable to the NPDB.

CHAPTER 2

12 Signs of a Sham Peer Review

Sham Peer Review is always a malicious "corrective action" proceeding commenced by a hospital medical staff against a physician to discipline the physician This is often motivated by concerns other than the quality of patient care – such as hospital politics, competitive advantage or retaliation.

There are twelve telltale signs that individually and collectively may indicate a situation of malicious Peer Review.

1. A doctor with a good work history and reputation is suddenly deemed to have questionable performance indicators. Absent intervening external causes such as recent substance abuse, mental illness or unusual stress of some kind, physicians usually do not suddenly "turn south" in terms of professional judgment and performance.

2. The presence of gunny sacking issues. Gunny sacking is the dredging up of old issues long since resolved to demonstrate present problems. While history can be important if it demonstrates a consistent pattern of misbehavior or uneven performance, old anecdotal grievances newly retrieved is reminiscent of a spouse who, as the

librarian of the other spouse's faults, raises old
grievances in new disagreements.

3. The existence of an "insider" clique of physicians
who fiercely maintain control of Peer Review and
credentialed positions and pass key medical staff
positions back and forth among themselves – while
excluding "outsiders".

4. The lack of clear, definitive standards in medical
staff bylaws for "disruptive conduct," denial or non-
renewal of privileges or other disciplinary measures.
This permits each physician participating in the Peer
Review process to assert his or her own "standards"
no matter how subjective to the process. *See Kiester v.
Humana Hospital Alaska, Inc.,*[2]

5. Medical staff acting in excess of authority or
violating the medical staff bylaws. Failure to follow the
letter of the procedures set forth in the investigative or
hearing process frequently underscores a separate
agenda.

---

[2] 843 P.2d 1219 (Alaska, 1992) (basic principles of due
process of law require that criteria established for
granting or denying of hospital privileges to physicians
not be vague and ambiguous, and that as established,
they be applied objectively.)

6. The existence of personal animus on the part of those participating in the investigative or hearing process is a clear marker of retaliatory intent.

7. The existence of a conflict of interest on the part of those measuring or participating in the Peer Review proceedings can violate fundamental conflict of interest principles – casting doubt on the genuineness of espoused quality of care concerns.

8. Minor issues of quality of care magnified beyond a reasonable expectation. Every professional makes mistakes and many are lucky when they do not precipitate major problems for their patients and clients. When a reviewing committee loses its perspective and elevates otherwise minor infractions into major violations, judgment becomes flawed and impaired.

9. The "piling on" of complaints. Rather than discrete, illuminating case issues the medical staff appears to throw every thinkable transgression, real or imagined, on the part of the physician against the wall with the non-transparent hope that something will stick.

10. Disparate and discriminatory treatment. When a physician on the "outside" is treated substantially different with respect to the intensity of scrutiny than a physician on the "inside," where it is clear that the insiders are not demanding from themselves and other insiders the same degree of practice

performance as the physician under review. This is seen most dramatically in the differential review treatment of two physicians involved in the same case.

11. In the failure to seek all relevant information concerning an issue before a rush to judgment – key physicians or nursing staff members not interviewed and the charts not carefully reviewed. The sample of cases reviewed in order to reach a judgment on competence is unduly narrow.[3]

12. The existence of only "a faint nod" in the proceedings towards a sincere concern for quality or safety of patient care. The lack of consistency in concern about quality of patient care can be a tip-off of a separate agenda or ulterior motive in the proceedings.

While true good faith Peer Review is an important function of medical staff physicians, the temptation to exploit its protections under the HealthCare Quality Improvement Act of 1996 can sometimes be overwhelming, particularly in small, closed communities of providers.

Vigilance over Sham Peer Review should be maintained to protect against the erosion of basic constitutional rights.

---

[3] See *Brown v. Presbyterian Healthcare Services*, 101 F.3d 1324 (10th Cir. 1996).

CHAPTER 3

Star Chamber Peer Review: Alive and Well?

When Congress passed the HealthCare Quality Improvement Act of 1996, it was responding to a level of hysteria among medical professionals concerning the prospect of rapacious lawyers suing doctors for anti-trust violations resulting from Peer Review activities.

The United States Supreme Court was about to affirm in *Patrick v. Bourget,*[4] where a physician had just received a substantial verdict against a number of Astoria, Oregon physicians, who had conspired to expel their former colleague from the medical staff of a hospital after he left their group.

Alarm was rife in the land that doctors would not be willing to perform effective Peer Review if they were not protected from rapacious lawyers hired by peer-reviewed physicians. (Rapacious lawyers are rapacious lawyers regardless of whether patients or other doctors hire them.)

The resulting statute created the National Practitioner Data Bank (NPDB), set minimal standards for Peer Review due process, provided qualified immunity for

---

[4] 486 U.S. 100 (1988),

participating physicians, and endowed Peer Review proceedings with a cloak of confidentiality.

On the surface this looked like a good idea to protect the public from venal and incompetent doctors, while protecting the integrity of the Peer Review process.

The problem however, is that this can create an enormous potential for abuse in the hands of "insider" physicians bent on maintaining personal power and economic advantage over their fellow colleagues. This is much akin to allowing the fox to guard the hen house, by permitting politically astute doctors to harness the power to destroy another physician's practice and livelihood in order to protect themselves, maintain power and to make money.

What was of such concern in the Patrick case anyway? In that case the defendants had axes to grind with Dr. Patrick and should not have been sitting in judgment on their peer in the first place.

Two recent cases demonstrate the type of conduct that all too frequently takes place in these kinds of proceedings behind closed doors. Dr. John Ulrich, Jr. obtained a $4.3M verdict against Laguna Honda hospital and others.

The defendants placed him under investigation for incompetence after he complained about patient care concerns in the hospital. Subsequently, he was reported to the National Practitioner Data Bank and spent years trying to get his name cleared from the Data Bank.

Three physicians obtained a $5.5M verdict against Yale University resulting from sanctions imposed by the chief of their section when the doctors complained about new hospital policies affecting patient care.[5] These kinds of cases are all too frequently dismissed because of the immunity and confidentiality provisions of HCQIA.

HCQIA should be amended to eliminate the confidentiality provisions of the Peer Review process, if requested by the affected physician.

If the Peer Review process is being pursued in good faith as required for immunity, there should be no need to include the "belt and suspenders" of both immunity and confidentiality. The process should be subjected to the "disinfectant" of sunshine while providing for the privacy and de-identification of patient records used in the proceedings

---

[5] See http:www.semmelweis.org/ref/080g.pdf

CHAPTER 4

Sham Peer Review and the Evolution of Immunity

Several years ago, as part of preparing an opening statement before a hospital "Peer Review" hearing in Wyoming, I tried to define the objective indicia of Sham Peer Review that I had observed over many cases that appeared and reappeared with some frequency in hospital privileges cases where the prosecution of charges seemed to be motivated by factors other than quality of patient care.

These motivators sometimes included hospital politics, jealousy, retaliation, turf wars, achievement of competitive advantage or just run away egos. Some entrenched medical staffs have a reputation for "eating their young."

I developed a list of twelve telltale signs, which taken individually or collectively, may suggest the presence of "Sham Peer Review" (that is, a bad faith Peer Review manipulated against a physician for a purpose other than the protection of patient safety.)

Prior to 1982, there was relatively little antitrust action in the healthcare field. Many believed there existed an informal "professional exemption" from antitrust scrutiny.

In 1982, the U.S. Supreme Court threw the medical profession into turmoil by finding that the Maricopa County Medical Society had engaged in illegal antitrust conduct by imposing a "maximum fee" schedule that its members would charge health plans. The case, *Arizona v. Maricopa County Medical Society*,[6] clearly established the application of antitrust laws to the medical profession.

The history of modern Peer Review relates back to the Supreme Court's decision six years later *in Patrick v. Burget*.

Dr. Patrick was a General and Vascular Surgeon in the small North Oregon coastal town of Astoria. The Astoria Clinic, a private physician group, dominated the only hospital in Astoria - Columbia Memorial Hospital. A majority of the hospital's medical staff were employees or partners at the Astoria Clinic. The clinic invited Dr. Patrick to join them, but he chose to remain an independent practitioner thereby competing with them.

Dr. Patrick immediately began to experience problems with the clinic, which essentially shunned him. He received virtually no referrals from the clinic even though the clinic did not always have a surgeon available. Instead, the clinic referred patients to outside surgeons over fifty miles away, rather than sending them to Dr. Patrick.

Subsequently, members of the Astoria Clinic group commenced a Peer Review investigation of Dr. Patrick, reviewing what they asserted was

---

[6] 457 U.S. 332(1982),

substandard quality of care below the professional standard.

Dr. Patrick filed suit in federal court alleging that the defendants had violated Section 1 (combination in restraint of trade) and Section 2 (monopolization) of the Sherman Antitrust Act by using the hospital Peer Review process to reduce competition rather than to improve patient care.

The court entered judgment against the defendants in the amount of $650,000 (then tripled under the Sherman Act). The U.S. 9th Circuit Court of Appeals reversed the judgment on the grounds that the defendants were immune from antitrust liability under the "state action" doctrine of *Parker v. Brown,* [7] because Oregon had articulated a policy in favor of Peer Review and actively supervised it to the extent that the Peer Review process was the action of the state, which was not subject to scrutiny.

On further appeal, the United States Supreme Court disagreed, finding that Oregon failed to meet the "active supervision" of the Parker exemption because there was no evidence that state officials reviewed or could review private decisions regarding hospital privileges.

The defendants and various "amici" or "friends of the court" participants including the American Medical Association, argued that Peer Review immunity is essential to the provision of quality medical care and that the ominous threat of antitrust liability would chill

---

[7] 317 U.S. 341

physicians' open and active participation in Peer Review.

Justice Marshall for the Supreme Court noted that the argument "Essentially challenges the wisdom of applying the antitrust laws to the sphere of medical care," which he opined should be best directed to the legislature. There followed a hue and cry for legislative and other protections for the Peer Review process to protect the integrity (or some would argue the lack of integrity) in the medical Peer Review system.

THE HEALTHCARE QUALITY IMPROVEMENT (HQCIA) ACT OF 1986; [8]

While the *Patrick v. Burget* case was winding its way toward the U.S. Supreme Court, Congress was concerned about the rise in medical malpractice cases and the apparent ineffectiveness of Peer Review, which allowed incompetent physicians to move from state to state with impunity when they were professionally "outed". Congress was also concerned about the impact the Patrick case would have on the willingness of physicians to sit on Peer Review panels because of the potential liability. In the decade before 1987, more medical malpractice cases were filed than in the entire prior history of tort law. The American Medical Association lobbied very hard for both confidentiality in Peer Review and immunity for the participants. In turn, Congressman Ron Wyden

---

[8] 42 U.S.C. 11101-11152 ("HCQIA")

of Oregon introduced HCQIA legislation (Patrick was an Oregon case).

As a result the HCQIA:

(1) established the National Practitioner Data Bank (the NPDB) as a repository for reports of adverse professional Peer Review actions and for malpractice payments;

(2) provided for mandatory reporting by hospitals, state medical boards and insurance companies of adverse actions with regards to licensing, hospital privileges and malpractice settlements to the NPDB;

(3) required all hospitals credentialing physicians to query the NPDB at least biennially and;

(4) provided for qualified immunity for Peer Review participants who met the standards of Section 11112 of HCQIA.

The initial HCQIA bill, H.R. 5110, contained a provision that provided Blanket Immunity from suit. Unlike Blanket Immunity, Qualified Immunity is generally perceived as immunity from damages absent some showing of bad faith or malice. Some legislators were concerned that complete immunity from suit would raise the specter of large-scale abuse of the process for ulterior poses. A subsequent bill, H.R. 5540 replaced the Blanket Immunity with the Qualified Immunity provisions. The standards for immunity were intended to be objective rather than subjective in their application.

Under Qualified Immunity, in order for immunity to attach to a professional review action, it must be taken;

(1) In the reasonable belief that the action was in the furtherance of quality healthcare;

(2) After a reasonable effort to obtain the facts of the matter;

(3) After adequate notice and hearing procedures are forwarded to the physician involved or after such other procedures as fair to the physician under the circumstances; and;

(4) In the reasonable belief that the action was warranted by the facts known after such reasonable effort to obtain facts and after meeting the requirements of (3) above.

HCQIA at Section 11112(a) provided that the HCQIA standards "will be satisfied if the reviewers, with the information available to them at the time of the professional review action, would reasonably have concluded that their action would restrict incompetent behavior or would protect patients" and that "[a] professional review action shall be presumed to have met the [4 HCQIA] standards... unless the presumption is rebutted by a preponderance of the evidence."

Section 11112(b) of HCQIA provides a list of procedures that if undertaken by the reviewing body would meet the "adequate notice and hearing requirements" of condition (3) in the immunity requirements.

However, there is an important "catch" in the same section, which takes away most of the protections which the "due process" provisions provide.

> *A professional review body's failure to meet the conditions described in this subjection shall not, in itself, constitute a failure to meet the standards of subsection (a)(3).* [9]

The vast majority of cases for damages brought against hospital Peer Review members are dismissed by courts on motions for Summary Judgment.

The irony is that a panel of incompetent doctors with long histories of malpractice can sit in judgment of a physician who is unable to show that he or she is being discriminated against in bad faith by accusers who are substantially less competent because their own capabilities and malpractice experience cannot be considered as it would be irrelevant if there is any

---

[9] 42 U.S.C. Sec. 11112 (b).

colorable basis for the complaint against the physician scrutinized. [10]

HCQIA immunity as written and widely interpreted presents a long uphill slog for any single physician in any attempt to recover damages for Sham Peer Review. It presents the opportunity for some to take manipulation in workplace politics to unconscionable levels of impunity.

---

[10] See *Floyd T. Bryan v. James E. Holmes Regional Medical Center*, 33 F. 3d 1318 (11th Cir. 1994)("The test is an objective one, so bad faith is immaterial. The real issue is the sufficiency of the basis for the [Hospital's] actions.")

CHAPTER 5

Top Ten "No Immunity" Sham Peer Review Cases

This series describes the top ten "no immunity" Sham Peer Review cases where defendants' motions for Summary Judgment based upon the immunity provided under the HealthCare Quality Improvement Act of 1986, 42 U.S.C. Sec. 11112 ("HCQIA") were denied in state or federal courts.

No. 10: *Islami v. Covenant Medical Center, Inc. et. al.* [11]

Dr. Islami had a contract to provide vascular lab services for patients at the defendant hospital. He was by all accounts an excellent technical surgeon. It was alleged by some members of the medical staff including some of his competitors affiliated with the hospital's own laboratory that he either used poor judgment or that surgery was not indicated in a number of his cases.

He was notified after the fact that a determination had been made to summarily suspend him and to apply 100% review, mandatory consultations and mandatory second opinions on his cases.

Dr. Islami brought an action alleging the hospital's breach of contract in failing to adhere to its own bylaws requiring a fair hearing before adverse actions against his privileges, tort and antitrust claims.

The defendants sought Summary Judgment based upon HCQIA Immunity. The court refused to apply the immunity provisions as a matter of law, but rather ruled that the jury could determine whether the actions of the defendants met the due process requirements of HCQIA.

> *That act also recognizes, however, that suspension of a doctor's staff privileges can have a devastating effect upon a medical professional. Consequently, the*

---

[11] 822 F. Supp. 1361 (N.D. Iowa 1992).

act has set up specific procedural safeguards which must be given to the doctor before the hospital and physician members of the Peer Review process are afforded the benefits of the immunity provisions. This court cannot say as a matter of law that the Peer Review process in this case accorded Dr. Islami all of the due process rights to which he is entitled. Consequently, this matter will have to be submitted to a jury.

The court took notice of the earlier and important case of *Austin v. McNamara, 979 F.2d 728 (1992)* wherein the 9th Circuit decided that the question of immunity could be determined at Summary Judgment.

Austin found that a somewhat nontraditional standard for Summary Judgment applied in immunity cases under HCQIA. The Austin court found that because Section 11112(a) provides a rebuttable presumption of immunity the Summary Judgment inquiry is best stated as follows:

"Might a reasonable jury, viewing the facts in the best light for [the plaintiff], conclude that he has shown, by a preponderance of the evidence, that the defendants' actions are outside the scope of Section 11112(a)."

The Iowa court went on to note that while Austin indicated that the question of immunity may be determined at the Summary Judgment stage, it also may be left for trial if the standard cannot be satisfied.

The Austin case is one of the most frequently cited cases in support of the grant of Summary Judgment under Section 11112(a). Islami was one of the first cases to assert a reasonable caution because of the potential impact of HCQIA on a physician's livelihood.

No. 9: *Hussein, M.D. v. Duncan Regional Hospital, Inc. d/b/a Duncan Regional Hospital, et. al.*[12]

Duncan Regional Hospital, Inc. granted Dr. Hussein, a Radiologist, locum tenens privileges for a two-week period in April of 2004. He provided radiological services, reading radiographic films. Shortly after beginning, he abruptly left the hospital, asserting that the hospital was requesting that he read too many films a day, which put patient safety at high risk. Following meetings of the hospital Credentials Committee, the Medical Executive Committee and the hospital Board of Directors, the hospital terminated his privileges and reported him to the National Practitioner Data Bank. It was undisputed that the hospital provided no notice or opportunity for Dr. Hussein to be heard prior to the report.

He filed suit for Interference, Defamation, Intentional Infliction of Emotional Distress and Gross Negligence.

The court held that the hospital's failure to provide any form of notice or opportunity to be heard barred the application of immunity for the hospital under HCQIA.

> *As it is undisputed that Dr. Hussein was not given any notice or opportunity to be heard prior to the hospital's report to the NPDB, the court concludes that defendants are not entitled to immunity under... HCQIA... To the extent that plaintiff's motion for Summary Judgment*

---

[12] Civ. No. 5-07-0439 F (W.D. Okla., May 1, 2009).

requests such a determination, the motion will be granted.[13]

---

[13] Ibid at page 7 of 10.

No. 8: *Estate of Blume v Marion Health Center* [14]

A curious set of facts exists in the case of *Estate of Horst G. Blume and Headache & Pain Control Center, P.C., v. Marion Health Center and its successor in interest, Mercy Medical Center-Sioux City*, filed in the United States District Court for the Northern District of Iowa, Western Division on March 14, 2007.

The case arose out of the summary suspension of Dr. Blume from practice on December 2, 1998 apparently based upon some incident reports. The Federal District Court held that the hospital failed to provide Dr. Blume with a hearing on his suspension and therefore failed to qualify for the statutory requirements for immunity under the HCQIA. The circumstances surrounding the failure to provide a hearing are unusual.

Dr. Blume requested a hearing after he received notice from the hospital of his suspension. A number of procedural delays followed. Dr. Blume's attorney was barred from appearing at a hearing at the hospital.

The hospital "unreasonably delayed" turning over the incident reports that were the basis for the suspension to Dr. Blume and his attorney, arguing that the discovery request was "overbroad". Other correspondence existed between the hospital and Dr.

---

[14] 503 F. SUPP. 2D 1103 (N.D. IOWA, 2007), VACATED 516 F 3D 705 (8TH CIR. 2008)

Blume in which the hospital repeatedly asked when Dr. Blume wanted his hearing, but apparently made no attempt to set it over time.

The court repeatedly indicated that Dr. Blume was only required to ask for the hearing once. There is also a fuzzy reference to the fact that the court excluded damages to Dr. Blume for the period in which he had obtained an injunction prohibiting a hearing against him in Woodberry County.

Dr. Blume filed suit against the hospital on December 2nd, 2003, for anti-trust, violation of due process, interference and other torts. All were dismissed except a Breach of Contract claim.

The court held on a Summary Judgment motion for Dr. Blume that under Iowa law, the medical staff bylaws right to a hearing and other procedures was a contract and that the hospital breached the same by not providing Dr. Blume with a hearing.

A jury later found damages in the amount of $146,025, which the trial court upheld following post trial motions.

The moral of the case seems to be that if a suspended physician requests a hearing in a timely manner to which he or she is entitled under the medical staff bylaws, a hospital should make sure the physician gets that hearing, even if he or she fails to respond to requests as to when it is desired.

No. 7: In Re: Peer Review Action [15]

This case arose out of a Peer Review action against an anonymous physician who appears to have been a surgeon imposed with a 120 day suspension and five years' probation for Disruptive Conduct.

The hospital had a Disruptive Physician policy that provided for graduated sanctions with notice and the opportunity to develop conflict resolution skills.

The hospital's Vice-President of Medical Services commenced an investigation of the physician on the basis of claims of Disruptive Conduct with only one specific date mentioned where the physician was alleged to have been "uncompromising with an anesthesiologist," and where he or she lost his or her temper and let forth a stream of profanity.

During the process of addressing this issue before a Hearing Committee, the Review Committee found ample evidence of disruptive behavior but did not address the physician's concern about the lack of notice and opportunity to self- correct.

The Review Committee under the bylaws, was required to issue a written report stating the grounds for sanctions, but only issued a one-page Conclusionary Summary, citing no specifics. The physician requested detailed specifics so that the

---

[15] 749 N.W. 2d 822 (Minn. Ct. App 2008)

allegedly disruptive physician could answer the charges in a written format, which he was entitled to do. The hospital only redirected back to the one-page summary.

The physician filed a lawsuit seeking an injunction for Breach of Contract and Failure to Follow the Rules, which the trial court granted.

The hospital argued that it was immune from the imposition of an injunction under HCQIA and state law. The court dismissed the hospital's HCQIA immunity defense on the basis that there is no such Immunity from Injunctive Relief as the statute specifically refers to Immunity from Damages alone.

The court also dismissed the immunity claim under state law that can apply to injunctions.

> Hospital also claims immunity from Physician's temporary injunction under state law. Whether a party is entitled to statutory immunity is a question of law, which is subject to de novo review. Conlin v. City of St. Paul, 605 N.W.2d 396, 400 (Minn.2000). Minnesota law provides immunity to hospitals from damages or other relief in any action brought by a person subject to a peer-review inquiry. Unlike HCQIA, discussed above, state-law immunity extends to injunctive relief. Compare... with 42 U.S.C... 1111(a). However, a hospital forfeits its state-law immunity if its peer-review process was motivated by malice toward the subject of a peer-review

inquiry... The Minnesota Supreme Court has defined malice in the context of statutory immunity as nothing more than the intentional doing of a wrongful act without legal justification or excuse, or, otherwise stated, the willful violation of a known right.[16]

---

[16] Ibid at page 7 of 10.

No. 6: *Peper v. St. Mary's Hospital and Medical Center* [17]

In Peper, the Colorado Court of Appeals held that St. Mary's (a Colorado hospital) and its medical staff physicians, who revoked the plaintiff's hospital privileges without notice or a hearing, failed to establish grounds for immunity under the HealthCare Quality Improvement Act of 1986. Dr. Peper is a Cardiothoracic Surgeon who was appointed and reappointed to the "provisional actual medical staff of St. Mary's Hospital."

At about the time of his reappointment, the hospital began a secret review of nineteen of Dr. Peper's cases. An external reviewer asserted the presence of provisions that suggested the possibility of problems with surgical techniques and/or judgment.

On February 15, 2003, without prior notice, St. Mary summarily revoked Dr. Peper's privileges asserting "in-depth analysis demonstrated a pattern of consistently excessive cross-clamp times as well as several cases of care falling below generally accepted standards of practice." The hospital notified Dr. Peper that the medical bylaws did not provide for a hearing or appeal for provisional physicians.

In an earlier appeal, the Colorado Court of Appeals held that there was no immunity because of the hospital's inadequate notice and hearing provisions

---

[17] 207 P. 3d 881 (Colo. App. 2008).

under HCQIA and remanded the matter to the trial
court for the determination of whether Dr. Peper
waived his right to a hearing when he agreed to
accept provisional privileges under the bylaws. The
trial court granted Summary Judgment in favor of the
hospital and other defendants on remand because of
a waiver of rights.

The Court of Appeals again reversed:

> On the merits, we hold defendants are
> not entitled to HCQIA immunity because
> any agreement to be bound by hospital
> bylaws was legally insufficient to wave
> statutory due process rights under the
> third HCQIA standard.[18]

In the absence of an express and knowing waiver of
rights by a physician, the court ruled that regardless
of its bylaws, the hospital and its Peer Review
participants must comply with HCQIA's conditions for
immunity before they can obtain immunity.

> They provided Dr. Peper no opportunity
> to be heard before revoking his
> privileges and reporting him to the state
> medical board and the national data
> bank nor have defendants ever claimed
> there was some health emergency
> requiring immediate suspension of Dr.

---

[18] Ibid at 885.

Peper's privileges under 42 U.S.C. §
11112(c).[19]

The bylaws may impose contractual obligations on both sides, but do not inferentially trump statutory rights.

---

[19] Ibid at 887.

No. 5: *Jeung v. McKrow* [20]

Dr. Jeung was a surgeon of Korean descent who practiced at Hill and Dale Hospital in the Eastern District of Michigan, Northern Division. Denise McKrow was the hospital administrator. More than half of the medical staff at the hospital was non-caucasian. Dr. Jeung accused McKrow of efforts to bring in more Caucasian physicians including surgeons who would be retained as employees of the hospital.

The hospital received complaints that Dr. Jeung engaged in abusive treatment of nurses at the hospital and there were concerns expressed about his management style and interpersonal relationship skills. An independent physician, hired by the Board to evaluate the circumstances, opined that he thought McKrow was "out to get" Dr. Jeung.

The hospital, at a point, summarily suspended Dr. Jeung's surgical privileges and a Review Organization hired by the administration to review Dr. Jeung stated that he had a "significantly more aggressive practice pattern" than other surgeons.

Dr. Jeung showed up at his fair hearing with a number of experts of his own, but the hearing panel tried to exclude them from the proceedings. The hospital's attorney objected because he had not asked his experts to be present for the entire proceedings.

---

[20] 264 F. Supp 2d 557 (E.D. Mich. 2003)

When Dr. Jeung's experts refused to leave, the panel closed down the proceedings and determined that Dr. Jeung failed to proceed without good cause and waived his rights. Dr. Jeung sued for Breach of Contract and Violations of 42 U.S.C. Sec. 1981 and 1983 (civil rights).

The defendants claimed, inter alia, that they were entitled to immunity. The district court judge found that immunity under HCQIA did not apply for two reasons. First, by the terms of the Act, immunity does not apply to civil rights claims, and second, the hospital failed to comply with fair procedure requirements of HCQIA when it chose to shut down the hearing. HCQIA provides for Forfeiture of Notice and Fair Procedure Rights only when the "physician fails, without good cause, to appear."

The court noted that there were no hospital rules requiring the sequestration of experts and the general practice was for them to attend to more fully grasp the issues upon which they would be opining

No. 4: *Fullerton v. Florida Medical Association, Inc.* [21]

Dr. John Fullerton is a physician and Medical Malpractice expert witness. He is licensed to practice in Florida and California. but lived and practiced primarily in California. He is not a member of the Florida Medical Association (FMA). Dr. Fullerton testified in Florida in a medical malpractice case brought against Drs. Jonathan B. Wrach, Pravinchandra Zala and Joseph O. Krebs.

After a judgment in their favor, the doctors filed a complaint with the FMA asserting that Dr. Fullerton's opinion testimony fell below reasonable professional standards and was made for the sole purpose of propagating a frivolous lawsuit for financial gain.

Dr. Fullerton then filed suit against the three doctors and the FMA. He alleged the statements in their complaint were false and were submitted for processing by the FMA's Expert Witness Committee of its Council on Ethical and Judicial Affairs, which he alleged was organized for the purpose of "intimidating, hindering, and deterring persons, including plaintiff Fullerton, from appearing as expert witnesses on behalf of plaintiffs in cases involving Medical Malpractice."

He also claimed to have suffered damages and irreparable harm to his reputation. The trial court

---

[21] 938 So. 2d 587 (Fla. Dist Ct, App. 2006)

granted the defendants' motion for Summary Judgment on the basis that the Florida Peer Review statute and HCQIA barred Fullerton's claims in the absence of proof of intentional fraud. A Florida Appellate Court reversed the trial court.

The court held,

> In our judgment, because neither Florida's peer-review statutes nor the HCQIA clearly and unambiguously expresses the legislative intent that such testimony should be scrutinized by Peer Review, we conclude the statutes provide no immunity to the defendants.[22]

The court held that both the state and federal statute were intended to provide immunity for the Peer Review of physicians engaged in the rendering of professional services to a patient.

> It appears from our examination of the above statutes that the term professional review action, as it relates to a formal decision of a review body to take or not take action, encompasses the review of the professional conduct of a physician that might affect his or her patient's health, with the result that his or her right to clinical privileges or membership in a professional society

---

[22] Ibid at 591.

could be impacted. Nothing in the provision of the above statute, however, expressly or reasonably implies the professional body is empowered to review the quality of a physician's testimony in a medical-malpractice proceeding.[23]

The court acknowledged that its opinion was contrary to that of the U.S. 7th Circuit Court of Appeals. (*See Austin v. American Association of Neurological Surgeons,*[24]) with which it specifically disagreed.

The court further distinguished Austin, noting that unlike in Austin, Dr. Fullerton was not a member of the FMA and that the FMA had "no cause under the circumstances to subject Dr. Fullerton to its discipline."

---

[23] Ibid at 594.
[24] 253 F. 3d 967 (7th Cir. 2001)

44

No. 3: *Royal Benson, M.D. v. St. Joseph Regional Medical Center* [25]

This is not strictly an immunity case, but is important because of the court's ruling that the professional records of the Peer Reviewers was relevant to the plaintiff's antitrust claim.

Many cases hold that the record of Peer Reviewers is irrelevant in Peer Review proceedings because the sole issue is whether the presumptively "objective" criteria in evaluating the subject physician is overcome, not the subjective issue of ulterior motive that would be proven by selective prosecution of Peer Review actions.

On May 1, 2006, a federal district court in Houston, Texas, held that disparate treatment of a physician in Peer Review was relevant to the physician's antitrust case. In *Royal Benson, M.D.,* Judge Keith P. Ellison ruled that Dr. Benson was entitled to pursue discovery of discriminatory treatment of him in Peer Review by sustaining his request that St. Joseph Regional Medical Center produce Peer Review cases of physicians other than himself who went through Peer Review proceedings at St. Joseph.

Judge Ellison, acknowledged the validity of St. Joseph's argument that the relevant issue in the Peer Review proceedings was whether a physician's Peer

---

[25] (C.A. H-04-04323) (Memorandum and Order, May 1, 2006)

Reviews could reasonably have concluded that Dr. Benson provided substandard care. (See *Willman v. Hartland Hospital East*[26])

Judge Ellison found, however, that this was not the only issue relevant to the existence of anti-competitive conduct.

> *"On the contrary, an analysis of how Defendants treated Dr. Benson in the Peer Review process may be quite relevant to Plaintiff's claims that Defendants acted with anti-competitive intent. If Defendants in fact treated Dr. Benson more harshly than other physicians, this would seem to lend support to Plaintiffs' contention that Defendants acted with intent to remove Dr. Benson as a competitor in the Brazos County OB/Gyn market."*[27]

Hospitals and their medical staffs frequently assert in Post Privileges Termination legal proceedings that the only issue is whether the hearing panel could reasonably conclude that the physician practices substandard medicine justifying the restriction or elimination of his privileges.[28]

---

[26] 34 F.3d 605, 610-11 (8th Cir. 1994).
[27] *Op. Cit* at p. 2 0f 5.
[28] See *Smith v. Ricks*,31 F.3d 1478 (9th Cir. 1994); *Pamituan v. Nanticoke Memorial Hospital*, 192 F 3d 378 (3d Cir. 1999) and *Morgan v. Peacehealth*, 14 P 3d 773 (Wash. App. 2000).

Notwithstanding, the lack of consistency and evenhandedness in the Peer Review of hospital physicians represents potentially compelling evidence of intent to commit an antitrust violation or to violate the civil rights of a physician.

In Benson, the court ordered the hospital to produce all of the underlying cases in the hospital Peer Review of other physicians in order to permit Dr. Benson to do a comparative analysis of Peer Review of others compared to his own.

One of the major problems for hospitals in Peer Review actions is the lack of articulated standards for removing or non-renewal of medical staff privileges. In the absence of civil articulated and defined standards, each physician performing Peer Review is free to apply his or her own personal standards.

In such circumstances, it is easy for personal agendas or animus to intervene in the result against an unpopular or politically marginalized physician. It is also true that such a situation would adhere to the benefit of a popular and politically astute member of the staff.

A hospital would be well-advised to assure that its medical staff develop clear and explicit standards for determining privileges in its facilities and require that all Peer Review cases to be measured against the adopted standards, not only to provide effective due process of law but to insulate the organization from claims of disparate treatment. The court in Benson underscored that:

> *This view, that disparate treatment in the Peer Review process is relevant to claims of anti-competitive conduct, is also compatible with the decisions of other courts on the issue of Peer Review discovery. Memorial Hospital v. Shadur, for example, invalidated a physician's claim that a disciplinary proceeding against him was a sham intended only as a means of restraining trade.* [29]

To prove this allegation the court found that the physician needed to produce "evidence that other physicians with comparable or worse records than his" were not similarly disciplined.[30]

Similarly, in *Swarthmore Radiation Oncology v. Lanes*,[31] the court recognized that "where plaintiff's theory turns on comparison of how the defendants treated similarly situated physicians, staff privileges records are unquestionably relevant." Consistency and fairness in the application of Peer Review are the best defenses."

Unfortunately for Dr. Benson, the later dismissal of his case was ultimately affirmed by the 5th Circuit U.S.

---

[29] 664 F.2d 1058, 1062-1063 (7th Cir. 1981)
[30] Id. at 1063.
[31] 1993 WL 17722 at 1 (E.D. Pa. 1993).

Court of Appeals on a Summary Determination. The court ruled that he had now shown antitrust damages to competition. [32]

---

[32] 575 F. 3d 542 (5th Cir. 2009)

No. 2: *Clark v. Columbia/HCA Information Services, Inc.* [33]

Dr. Clark was a Child Psychiatrist with privileges at West Hills Hospital in Reno owned by Columbia/HCA.

The medical staff made him the subject of Peer Review for "disruptive conduct" because he complained to outside third parties about the quality of psychiatric care provided to children in the hospital, and that the hospital had policies mandating premature discharges of patients when their insurance money ran out.

The hospital raised other quality of care issues, but the prosecution of the Peer Review issues centered on his so-called disruptive conduct or whistle-blowing.

He first filed an Antitrust claim in federal court where he was dismissed because of a lack of evidence to support those claims. The federal judge indicated that his claims would probably be barred by HCQIA immunity anyway.

Dr. Clark was persistent and re-filed his state law claims in state court where he was dismissed again based on grounds of HCQIA immunity. He appealed to the Nevada Supreme Court, which took a different turn. After noting the paucity of cases refusing to grant HCQIA immunity, the court found that his

---

[33] 25 P 3d 215 (Nev. 2001).

whistle-blowing circumstances were unique and compelling.

> *[T]he findings of the hospital reflect that the reason for his dismissal was his apparently good faith reporting of perceived improper hospital conduct to the appropriate outside agencies or whistleblowing. The reports were apparently made to improve the quality of healthcare at the hospital. Revoking Clark's privileges based on this whistleblowing activity does not objectively further quality healthcare under S 11112(a)(1); thus, respondents are not entitled to immunity as a matter of law for their decision to revoke Clark's staff privileges.*[34]

Clark underscores the paradigmatic use of Sham Peer Review to quiet "disruptive physicians" trying to fix the system.

---

[34] Ibid at 222.

No. 1: *Brown v. Presbyterian Healthcare Services et al.* [35]

This case arose in the state of New Mexico. The plaintiff, Arlene M. Brown, M.D. was a family practice physician in Riodoso, NM. Also practicing in Riodoso was Dr. Vickie Williams, an OB/Gyn Physician and an economic competitor of Dr. Brown, who participated in a Peer Review of three patients treated by Dr. Brown.

She expressed concerns to Lincoln County Medical Center's administrator about the quality of care provided by Dr. Brown on three cases. Valerie Miller, the Hospital Administrator, instituted formal Peer Review proceedings against Dr. Brown. At a meeting with the hospital's Executive Committee, Dr. Brown agreed to consult with an Obstetrics Specialist with respect to "high risk" obstetrics cases.

Later the hospital asserted Dr. Brown breached her agreement with the hospital. A Peer Review panel recommended termination of her agreement and the hospital submitted a report to the National Practitioner Data Bank under a code entitled "Incompetence/ medical malpractice/ negligence. The hospital, on request, refused to amend the report.

In 1992, another Family Practice physician, Dr. Reib, contacted the hospital about family practice in Riodoso and the hospital told him that they would offer him a financial incentive for his practice only if he

---

[35] 101 F.3d 1324 (10th Cir. 1996)

agreed not to work for Dr. Brown but instead work at the hospital in direct competition with Dr. Brown.

Dr. Brown filed suit in Federal District Court asserting Antitrust claims and ancillary state law claims of Interference and Defamation. The case went to a jury, which returned a verdict for Dr. Brown. The District Court reversed some of the award claims and both sides appealed. The Court of Appeals reinstated Dr. Brown's damages claims and rejected the defendants' claims that they should be adjudged immune under HCQIA.

The court noted that the Peer Review panel at the hospital agreed to terminate Dr. Brown's privileges on the basis of the review of only two cases.

The formal Peer Review hearing was held to determine whether Dr. Brown had agreed to seek consultation for high-risk obstetrical patients and if so, whether Dr. Brown had breached this agreement. During the hearing, Ms. Miller (the hospital administrator) outlined the hospital's position, and the panel reviewed the charts of two patients Dr. Brown treated.

The court determined that this effort was not sufficient to demonstrate that there was a "reasonable effort to obtain the facts" as required by HCQIA.[36]

> *Although the data bank report in this case listed the reason for Lincoln*

---

[36] 42 U.S.C. Sec. 11112(a).

County Medical Center's disciplinary action as "negligence / incompetence/ malpractice," the record reveals neither the review panel nor the hospital's Board of Trustees ever found Dr. Brown negligent, incompetent, or guilty of malpractice. Rather the review panel merely determined Dr. Brown breached her agreement to obtain appropriate consultation.[37]

Thus the record is replete with evidence tending to show Ms. Miller and Dr. Williams were the catalysts behind, or played a crucial role in every step of the proceedings against Dr. Brown.[38]

---

[37] Op. Cit. at 1333-1334.
[38] Ibid at 1335.

CHAPTER 6

The Scope of Peer Review Immunity

Attacking the Peer Review Process

in order to successfully attack or challenge a Peer Review action, a physician must be able to attack the fairness of the total Peer Review process.

The New Mexico Supreme Court recently reversed the denial of a motion for Summary Judgment by a hospital claiming immunity under the HealthCare Quality Improvement Act of 1986.

William K. Summers, M.D. brought an action for damages against Ardent Health Services, LLC and Lovelace Health System, Inc., claiming Defamation, Breach of Contract, Prima Facie Tort, and Tortious Interference with Prospective Contracts as a result of a hospital Peer Review action against him.

He claimed that hospital investigations resulting in the suspension of his internal medicine and psychiatry privileges were retaliatory and the result of his reporting questionable practices of hospital administrators.

Dr Summers challenged the hospital's requirement under HCQIA of demonstrating a reasonable effort to acquire the facts because one of two complaining witnesses asserting that he used sexually explicit and inappropriate language during consultations was not interviewed by any investigator.

One of two reviewing committees, in addition to reviewing the file of the non-interviewed complainant, reviewed the records of eleven of plaintiff's patients and found "a relatively high incidence of questionable medical decisions or treatments rendered and identified seven problems specific to individual patients and three general problems."

In *Summers v. Ardent Health Services, LLC and Lovelace Health System, Inc.*[39], the trial court ruled that Dr. Summers raised a judicable issue of fact in the failure of the investigators to interview the second complaint, prohibiting a grant of Summary Judgment in favor of the hospital.

The Supreme Court, noting the presumption of validity of investigation by a hospital claiming immunity and the inadequacy of part of the medical staff investigation, determined that in order to overcome the presumption in favor of immunity it is not enough for a physician to show bad faith or to attack a part of the process, but rather he or she must show that the fact-finding process was unreasonable in its totality.

---

[39] No. 32,202 (NM 2011)

HCQIA IMMUNITY CAN APPLY TO PEER REVIEW OF PRIVATE PHYSICIAN CONDUCT:

In the recent case of *Moore, MD v. Williamsburg Regional Hospital et al.,*[40] a Federal Court of Appeals addressed the issue of how far a hospital Peer Review can go in considering the private conduct of a physician in suspending his or her hospital privileges.

The physician, Dr. Moore, is a General Surgeon who performs surgery on both adults and children in his practice. Dr. Moore's private life spilled over into his professional life in a tragic and unresolved way.

The South Carolina Department of Social Services (DSS) took Dr. Moore's three adopted children into protective custody following allegations that his wife had physically abused the children.

Later, the Moore's adopted daughter made a complaint that she had been abused by both Dr. Moore and his wife. There were apparently at least three DSS investigations, two were inconclusive and a third resulted in a formal complaint being filed in a family court.

The DSS later filed a voluntary non-suit allegedly because of concerns about the trauma of the child in pursuing the Moores and the fact that their parenting rights had been terminated pursuant to an agreement with the Moores in the physical abuse case in which

---

[40] No. 07-1966 (4th Cir. 2009),

there was apparently a stipulation of some kind of physical abuse and neglect.

Meanwhile, the hospital learned of the abuse allegations and summarily suspended Dr. Moore's privileges after obtaining a copy of the DSS complaint which detailed the statements made by the child to DSS investigators and others.

Dr. Moore appealed the suspension through three levels of review. He faced the largely impossible position of proving a negative without the ability to confront his adopted daughter. He did provide a psychiatric profile that indicated that he did not present the diagnostic criteria of a pedophile.

Dr. Moore lost his appeals and filed an action in federal court alleging federal and state court claims. The district court dismissed his case on immunity under HCQIA immunity and other grounds. The focus of his appeal was that his suspension was not a "professional review action" under HCQIA because it referred to matters outside of the jurisdiction of the hospital.

The hospital argued that the scope of its potential review of a physician's private life was unlimited as it related to immunity. The court disagreed with the hospital that its jurisdiction for Peer Review was unlimited.

> *A surgeon whose personal life might not bear close scrutiny may nonetheless save lives with his talents in the operating room. Giving Peer Review bodies the discretion to suspend staff*

> *privileges and report physicians for largely private defalcations, is thus to arm those reviewers with a club that Congress did not provide.*[41]

The court, nevertheless, found that there was a "clear nexus between the alleged misconduct and the plaintiff's medical practice."

> *In no sense did Congress mean to encourage fishing expeditions into private behavior. A "professional review action" requires that the record reflect a clear nexus between the basis for an "action" or "recommendation" and a physician's medical practice. 42 U.S. C. § 11151(9).*[42]

The court determined that there was a legitimate and reasonable concern at the hospital about the connection between Dr. Moore's surgical practice with children and the allegations of abuse of his adopted daughter. The allegations and concerns were thus within the penumbra of a professional review action and immunity applied, assuming the notice and other due process procedures complied with HCQIA requirements.

> *Any statutory standard inescapably involves some difficult exercises in judgment and to deny decision-makers the right to exercise judgment in close*

[41] Ibid at 173.

[42] Ibid at 172

cases is to defeat the purpose of immunity.[43]

---

[43] Ibid at 175.

CHAPTER 7

Ten Critical Pro-Immunity Peer Review Cases

The ten following Pro-Immunity Peer Review cases are important as related to pro-immunity where courts have granted immunity to Peer Reviewers under HCQIA.

No. 10: *Reyes v. Wilson Memorial Hospital,* [44]

Dr. Reyes was a board-certified internist who did not get along with his colleagues at the hospital. Having been summarily suspended in a Peer Review process, he sued the hospital for antitrust violations and state law torts, to which the defendants raised the issue of immunity.

According to an affidavit filed by Dr. Reyes in opposition to a motion for Summary Judgment, he suffered the resentment of his fellow doctors because of the effect his method of practice had on the income of the defendants. Dr. Reyes occasionally referred patients to hospitals other than Wilson Memorial and to doctors other than those named as defendants. This practice caused the defendants to suffer a loss of income.

Dr. Reyes also performed minor surgeries and diagnostic tests in his own office, rather than referring his patients to surgeons at Wilson Memorial or having their tests performed there. These practices earned him the enmity of his fellow doctors at the hospital.

One of the defendants warned him on several occasions to stop these practices. Dr. Reyes believed that the defendants' professional review actions were taken because of his refusal to move to a new medical office building, his practice of making referrals out of the Sidney area, and the fact that he had a successful practice. Dr. Reyes claimed that he

---

[44] 102 F Supp. 2d 798 (S.D. Ohio, 1998).

lost many patients and contracts as a result of his suspension.

The trial court responded:

> *As the previous section makes clear, a plaintiff bears the crucial burden of producing evidence, which could negate the statutory presumption that an eligible entity has acted in accordance with section 11112(a). The courts, which have addressed the issue of immunity under the HCQIA have been unanimous in holding that a plaintiff cannot prove the "unreasonableness" of a defendant's actions by introducing evidence suggesting that a defendant acted in "bad faith." Rather, the courts have held that such evidence is irrelevant. A defendant's actions must be judged on an objective basis.* [45]

The court in granting the defendants' motion for Summary Judgment held that, to prevail on a motion for Summary Judgment by the defendants the plaintiff must demonstrate that there exists any issue as to whether the result reached by the Peer Review board was based on a "reasonable belief" that it "was in the furtherance of quality healthcare."

The court held that the reasons for a summary suspension can ultimately be wrong; that is not the test of whether there has been a violation. A genuine

---

[45] Ibid at 811.

issue of fact concerns must exist for the reasonableness of the defendant's belief.

No. 9: Sugarbaker v. SSM Healthcare, d/b/a St. Mary's Healthcare[46]

Dr. Sugarbaker was a General Surgeon practicing in Jefferson City, Missouri in 1995.

A member of the medical staff raised concerns about his surgical technique and timing and he received a precautionary suspension of his privileges when he refused to refrain from practice voluntarily.

A number of committees reviewed his performance. Although the executive committee sought to permanently terminate him, other committees opted for restrictions and monitoring.

He eventually lost all of his privileges in 1999 when he refused to abide by the conditions imposed on him.

Dr. Sugarbaker filed a federal anti-trust claim and ancillary state claims essentially asserting that he was the victim of a conspiracy to control the medical services market in Jefferson City.

The trial court ultimately dismissed his claim because of HCQIA immunity applied. Dr. Sugarbaker appealed to the U.S. 8th Circuit Court of Appeals. He asserted that the defendants were acting in bad faith, that they engaged in procedural errors and that the defendants kept moving the goal posts on the allegations of inferior performance after he effectively responded to each concern.

---

[46] 190 F. 3rd 905 (8th Cir. 1999)

66

The court responded:

> *We agree with the views of our sister circuits and now hold that bad faith on the part of the reviews is irrelevant to the objective inquiry under [HCQIA].*[47]

Dr. Sugarbaker also objected to the "shared counsel" between the Appellate Review Committee and the Executive Committee reviewing his performance and to two general surgeons [competitors] serving on one of the committees. The court ruled that he failed to preserve these complaints by contemporaneous objection. Regarding the shifting concerns the court held:

> *Dr. Sugarbaker contends that he was deprived of a "fair hearing due to the continually changing charges brought against him." We disagree. The fact that the Peer Reviewer's concerns shifted as the investigation continued does not alone undermine the fairness of the procedures employed. During each phase of the Peer Review process, St. Mary's notified Dr. Sugarbaker of his procedural rights under the hospital's bylaws. Before each hearing, St. Mary's notified Dr. Sugarbaker of its concerns.*[48]

Finally, Dr. Sugarbaker contends that he is at least entitled to injunctive relief but the court, noting that he

---

[47] Ibid at 914.
[48] Ibid at 915

failed to file a motion for Injunctive Relief, determined that he had abandoned it.

68

No. 8: *Gabaldoni, M.D. v. Washington County Hospital Association et al.* [49];

Dr. Gabaldoni, was an Obstetrician/Gynecologist practicing in Virginia. and a holder of hospital privileges at Washington County Hospital Association (WCHA).

In 1995 he applied for a two-year extension of his privileges. The WCHA Board of Trustees elected to deny his request for an extension of privileges and to terminate his existing privileges. Grounds given included his alteration of the chart of a patient who died while under his care; multiple grievances regarding clinical judgment and the number of malpractice complaints settled on his behalf.

The interesting thing about Dr. Gabaldoni's case is that he seemed to be politically connected with his medical staff colleagues, who tried to protect him.

This dispute seems to have arisen directly from the hospital Board of Trustees and not the medical staff. The Credentials Committee, the Medical Executive Committee and the Ad Hoc Hearing Committee all recommended that he be reappointed.

The Board of Trustees chose not to follow the recommendations of those committees, and Dr. Gabaldoni filed suit in federal court alleging contract and tort claims. The trial court dismissed his case on the basis of HCQIA immunity.

---

[49] 250 F. 3d 255 (4th Cir., 2001)

He appealed to the U.S. 4th Circuit Court of Appeals, which noted that because of the presumption of immunity it would need to apply an "unconventional standard in determining whether WCHA was entitled to Summary Judgment - whether a reasonable jury, viewing the facts in a light most favorable to Gabaldoni, could conclude that he had shown, by a preponderance of the evidence, that WCHA's actions fell outside the scope of [HCQIA immunity "objective" standards]."[50]

The main thrust of Dr. Gabaldoni's argument was that the Board of Trustees failed to undertake an independent investigation of its own before rejecting the recommendations of the other physician panels and therefore could not have been based upon a reasonable effort to obtain all of the facts.

The Court of Appeals responded:

> *The HCQIA does not require the ultimate decision-maker to investigate a matter independently, but requires only a "reasonable effort to obtain" the facts. Thus, it was permissible for the Board to rely on the reports and investigations of the various committees (including the hearing Committee which was expressly formed for this purpose) in rendering its decisions, so long as "the totality of the process leading up to the Board's 'professional review action"... evidenced*

---

[50] Ibid at 260.

> *a reasonable effort to obtain the facts of the matter.*[51]

The Board's corporate counsel had provided summaries of the evidence collected by the various committees to each Board member. Although they did not contain every fact at issue, there was no evidence suggesting that the summaries were materially insufficient or misleading.

---

[51] Ibid at 261.

No. 7: *Meyers v. Columbia/HCA Healthcare Corp.* [52]

Dr. Robert Meyers applied for and received provisional privileges at Logan Memorial Hospital in Russellville, Kentucky.

He applied for active privileges a year later and met resistance because of a history of disruptive conduct at other facilities, a less than candid disclosure of his past problems with medical staffs, and concerns over the quality of his care. Dr. Meyers admitted that he had a "personality problem".

The Hospital Board of Trustees appointed a Hearing Committee of non-physicians because of Dr. Meyer's complaints about competitors sitting on his investigation panels. The Board voted to deny him privileges because of his inability to work cooperatively with others and his failure to meet the ethical standards of the facility.

Dr. Meyers filed three separate lawsuits; one in federal court and two in state court. He appealed the dismissal of his federal court claim based on Antitrust, Contract and Tort claims. He argued that the defendants did not meet the objective criteria of Reasonable Belief, Reasonable Effort, and Fair Notice and Process required for HCQIA Immunity.

The court held that taking ad hoc and conclusionary shots at some, but not all of the evidence presented in

---

[52] 341 F 3d 461 (6th Cir., 2003)

the hearing was insufficient to overcome the presumption in favor of immunity.

Interestingly, Dr. Meyers argued that because the hearing panel was made up of lay persons (non-physicians) it could not be considered to be a professional review action and therefore immunity did not apply.

Unfortunately for Dr. Meyers, none of the review panel had been named as defendants. In any event, the court determined that Peer Review immunity was not limited to just physicians as a matter of law.

No. 6: *Brader v. Allegheny General Hospital* [53]

Dr. Brader, a surgeon with a history of disruptive conduct within Allegheny Hospital (AGH), tried to attack the dismissal of his lawsuit against the hospital by attacking the validity of data and conclusions set forth in several reports undertaken by outside and inside hospital reviewers concerning his preoperative and intraoperative judgment as a means of establishing bias on the part of the hospital decision-makers.

The court again warned that the standard under immunity has nothing to do with getting the facts right or wrong, it simply comes down to whether the defendants were operating in a reasonable belief that they were furthering quality healthcare and making reasonable efforts to gather the relevant facts.

> *We are unwilling to conclude that a failure to include absolutely every AGH patient in a quality assurance review, or one mistaken attribution in a host of records, undermines an otherwise thorough report. In addition, the ultimate decisions made... were not based exclusively on Diamond's or Ochsner's report, nor were the decisions based exclusively on an evaluation of Brader's surgical skills... Instead, these entities had before them ample evidence that Brader was a disruptive force at AGH and that he exercised poor judgment*

---

[53] 167 F. 3d 832 (3d Cir. 1999)

repeatedly in his surgical, teaching, and personal interactions. Brader has failed to produce sufficient evidence that AGH's various review panels could not reasonably have concluded that suspending Brader's privileges would be in the best interests of AGH's patients...[54]

---

[54] Ibid at 840.

No. 5: *Bryan v. James E. Holmes Regional Medical Center* [55]

Dr. Bryan received a $4.2M Breach of Contract award by a federal jury in the District Court. The U.S. 11th Circuit Court of Appeals reversed. Dr. Bryan was by all accounts an excellent surgeon, but an unpleasant human being. He was known to be a "volcanic tempered perfectionist," with an odd sense of humor. (He told a nurse that her patient had hanged himself in his room, to keep her on her toes.) The hospital and the medical staff tried a variety of graduated suspensions to try to curb Dr. Bryan's behavior. He had a penchant for slapping nurses on their hands when he disliked their performances. He collected over 50 written complaint reports from various staff.

Dr. Bryan claimed that he was terminated by the hospital Board of Trustees because of personal animus directed at him, not quality of patient care. He presented no evidence of animosity. He also objected to the fact that the Board made their decision without reviewing a transcript of his fair hearing. The court responded that he should have presented it to them himself if he thought it was important.

Dr. Bryan's argument did little to overcome the court's reluctance to overrule the decisions of a hospital board where any reasonable evidence supports a termination action.

> *Accordingly, as in all procedural due*
> *process cases, the role of federal courts*

---

[55] 33 F.3d 1318 (11th Cir. 1994).

"on review of such actions is not to substitute our judgment for that of the hospital's governing board or to reweigh the evidence regarding the renewal or termination of medical staff privileges"... No reasonable jury could conclude that Bryan had demonstrated, by a preponderance of the evidence, that the hospital board did not act in the "reasonable belief that the [termination] was warranted by the facts known after reasonable effort to obtain facts" as required by section [HCQIA].[56] (citations omitted.

---

[56] Ibid at 1370.

No. 4: *Austin v. McNamera* [57]

Dr. George Austin was a Neurosurgeon who received medical staff privileges at Santa Barbara Cottage Hospital. Dr. McNamera was the Chief of Staff at Cottage Hospital. Dr. Austin complained that he was attacked by other members of the medical staff in front of nurses and that other neurosurgeons at the hospital refused to cover for him. The medical staff commenced an investigation of his cases by members of the medical staff and two outside reviewers. The outside reviews were generally favorable to him despite some limited reservations. Three days after HCQIA became law, Dr. McNamera summarily suspended Dr. Austin for seven months. During his suspension, he continued his practice at other local hospitals where his privileges remained intact.

Following his termination, he obtained the right to a review by the hospital's Judicial Review Committee (JRC) They found that based on the facts presented that his suspension was "unreasonable." They did however impose some "appropriate conditions" along with the lifting of his suspension. Dr. Austin filed suit claiming that he was a victim of vicious and anticompetitive behavior by the medical staff and that based on the JRC decision his suspension was unreasonable, thus thwarting immunity under HCQIA. The court quoted a legislative committee report that the "reasonableness" standard was an objective one rendering "bad faith" irrelevant.

---

[57] 979 F.2d 728 (9th Cir., 1992)

Initially, the Committee considered a "good faith" standard for professional review actions. In response to concerns that "good faith" might be misinterpreted as requiring only a test of the subjective state of mind of the physicians conducting the professional review action, the Committee changed to a more objective "reasonable belief" standard. The Committee intends that this test will be satisfied if the reviewers, with the information available to them at the time of the professional review action, would reasonably have concluded that their actions would restrict incompetent behavior or would protect patients.[58]

The court, further, ruled that the JRC decision to include some limitation on his privileges justified a different type of "reasonableness" standard, under the objective rule.

Judge Pregerson dissented, primarily on the basis that the JRC finding of unreasonableness provided ample evidence that Dr. Austin's suspension was "unreasonable" and not entitled to the HCQIA immunity. He also noted that all of the conduct, save for the actual suspension, occurred before the

---

[58] Ibid at 734

enactment of HCQIA and that he disagreed with the decision of the other panelists to retroactively apply it.

No. 3: *Mathews v. Lancaster General Hospital* [59]

Dr. Mathews was an Orthopedic Surgeon with privileges at Lancaster General Hospital in Pennsylvania. He was scheduled as the assistant surgeon on a case that turned out poorly, but he was not present at the operation.

The Surgeon in Charge, Dr. Kent, punctured the patient's esophagus with a high-speed drill. He repaired the wound but there were later unfortunate sequelae. The hospital Peer Review investigation of Dr. Kent led to a review of Dr. Mathews' cases as well because there was an arrangement between Dr. Mathews and Dr. Kent to participate in each other's surgeries.

An exhaustive review of Dr. Mathews' cases by his hospital colleagues and an independent reviewer followed in which they found substantial deficiencies in many of Dr. Mathews' cases.

On September 16, 1993, the hospital Board of Directors voted to restrict Dr. Mathews' privileges to perform spine surgery as either primary or assisting surgeon. They also voted to require Dr. Mathews to obtain a second opinion or consultation before performing prosthetic joint surgery, arthroscopy, or hand or foot surgery for a period of 12 months. The Board notified Dr. Mathews of its decision by letter dated September 22, 1993, and informed him of his right to a fair hearing under Lancaster General

---

[59] 87 F.3d 624 (3rd Cir. 1996)

Hospital Medical Staff Bylaws. On October 26, 1993, Dr. Mathews requested a hearing, and the Board subsequently voted to suspend the restrictions on his privileges until a hearing could be held. Before the hearing was scheduled, however, Dr. Mathews filed his suit alleging Antitrust violations and various state law claims.

The trial court granted Summary Judgment in favor of the defendants based on HCQIA immunity. Dr. Mathews appealed the decision to the 3rd Circuit Court of Appeals, arguing that the defendants were engaged in a conspiracy to restrain his trade and that the hospital and the orthopedic physicians participating in the investigation were competitors of his. The court held that the mere participation by competitors in the investigation leading up to the Peer Review action did not run afoul of HCQIA. Even though HCQIA suggests that a hearing officer or individuals sitting on a hearing panel should not be in direct competition with the subject of a hearing, it poses no such restrictions on participants in other phases of the Peer Review process.

The court concluded:

> *Dr. Wilson, the outside reviewer, concluded that Dr. Mathews had provided substandard care in spine surgery cases. The Board then placed restrictions on Dr. Mathews' privileges to conduct spine surgery. Because these restrictions were tailored to address the*

healthcare concerns raised by the reports of the Rothacker Committee and Dr. Wilson, we believe the evidence supports the conclusion that the restrictions were imposed based on a reasonable belief that they were warranted by the facts known... While the conflicting expert reports raise an issue of fact as to the adequacy of care provided by Dr. Mathews, they do not rebut the presumption that the Board made its decision in the reasonable belief that it was warranted by the facts known. [60]

---

[60] Ibid at 638

No. 2: *Singh v. Blue Cross and Blue Shield, Inc. of Massachusetts* [61]

Dr. Singh, an internist, filed suit against Blue Cross and Blue Shield of Massachusetts and an independent consultant over a recommendation for his exclusion from insurance plans based on concerns over his allegedly excessive use of pain medication for chronic problems and unusually lengthy regimens of antibiotics for his patients. Dr. Singh sued for Breach of Contract, Tortious Interference with Business Relationships with Patients, Defamation and Violation of State Consumer Protection statutes. After a "fair hearing" his exclusion was reversed and he was reinstated as a provider in the insurer's system.

The trial court and the Court of Appeals agreed that his action should be dismissed both on their merits and on the HCQIA immunity defense.

> *The reversal of a Peer Review committee's recommendation by a higher level Peer Review panel does not indicate that the initial recommendation was made without a reasonable belief that the recommendation would further quality healthcare.* [62]

---

[61] 308 F. 3d 25 (1st Cir., 2002)
[62] Ibid at 41

The court looked to the attention to detail paid by the defendants to the healthcare issues as a basis for its determination that the "reasonable belief" standard was a bar to a damages claim.

> *Given the two audits and the level of attentions Dr. White gave to each chart he reviewed, no reasonable jury could find that Dr. Singh overcame the statutory resumption that Blue Cross engaged in a reasonable effort to obtain relevant facts.*[63]

---

[63] Ibid at 43.

No. 1: *Poliner v. Texas Health Systems* [64]

The 5th Circuit Court of Appeals reversed the $33M awarded the plaintiff in *Poliner v. Texas Health Systems*. The Poliner case raised a lot of eyebrows both because of the amount of the original damages award of $360M and its success in overcoming immunity claims under HCQIA. The trial court reduced the award to $33M prior to the appeal. Dr. Poliner, an Interventional Cardiologist, claimed that he was forced to agree to an abeyance of his privileges in lieu of a summary suspension and was prevented from performing procedures in the defendant's catheterization laboratory while an investigation was pending. He only identified about $10,000 in actual damages. His case went to a jury solely on defamation grounds.

The Court of Appeals found that HCQIA immunity applied to the defamation claims as well as to the hospital's legitimate concerns about an apparent deterioration in the quality of care provided by Dr. Poliner in the catheterization lab. The court found that the Peer Review action was taken in the reasonable belief that the action was in furtherance of quality healthcare.

The "reasonable belief" standard of HCQIA is satisfied if "the reviewers, with the information available to them at the time of the professional review action, would reasonably have concluded that

---

[64] 537 F 3d 368 (5th Cir., 2008)

> *their action would restrict incompetent behavior or would protect patients."* [65]

The court noted that it does not matter whether or not the conclusions reached by the Peer Review panel were in fact correct and that the good faith or bad faith of the reviewers is irrelevant, because of the objective nature of the test. The court determined that no reasonable observer could dispute the fact that the hospital made a reasonable effort to obtain the facts. The court recognized the potential for abuse of Peer Review, but suggested that injunctive or declaratory relief was the appropriate avenue for relief.

> *It bears emphasizing that this does not mean that hospitals and Peer Review committees that comply with the HCQIA's requirements are free to violate the applicable bylaws and state law. The HCQIA does not gainsay the potential for abuse of the Peer Review process. To the contrary, Congress limited the reach of immunity to money damages. The doors to the courts remain open to doctors who are subjected to unjustified or malicious Peer Review, and they may seek appropriate injunctions and declaratory relief in response to such treatment.* [66]

---

[65] Ibid at 378
[66] Ibid at 381

This suggestion provides relatively cold comfort given the cost of litigation these days. In some respects Dr. Poliner's initial success, given his relatively low actual damages, probably preordained this result. The court indicated that it didn't see any antitrust damages and that it probably would have reversed the judgment due to excessive damages being awarded.

Nor need we reach the compelling arguments that, at the very least, we would have to reverse and remand for a new trial because of the jury's excessive verdict and manifest trial errors. [67]

---

[67] Ibid at 385.

CHAPTER 8

The Disagreeable Doctor:
Disruptive or Disputative?

Most hospitals now have "Disruptive Physician" policies that provide for sanctions up to and including loss of privileges for physicians engaging in conduct that disrupts the aspirations and collegial harmony of a hospital.

The definition of what constitutes disruptive behavior in most of these policies is left so inordinately broad and so diaphanously vague as to render them effective tools for silencing responsible criticism and necessary patient advocacy by physicians or as a lever to maintain internal politics within the medical staff or as a vehicle to disable pesky economic competitors.

The penumbra of legitimate Peer Review concerning disruptive physician conduct should reasonably be defined by the immediacy of potential patient harm.

Let's take two typical, but very different, disruptive physician cases. In case one, the physician may be, as described by John-Henry Pfiffering, an "interpersonal hurricane with a calm eye when he or she feels in control and violent outbursts when he or she feels out of control." The physician, who constantly and publicly berates, blames and belittles nurses and other subordinates in an unjustified and inappropriate manner, falls into this pattern. This is frequently a narcissistic, but insecure, professional of the "kiss up and kick down" variety. This kind of behavior makes nurses and other staff reluctant to work with the physician or to reasonably communicate concerns lest they be subject to verbal or even physical retribution. Clearly the "does not play well with other children" appellation applies.

Abusive conduct leads to surgical or procedural team dysfunction in the hospital, which can translate into real and immediate patient harm. The hospital and its medical staff can and should act to suppress or control this kind of disruptive behavior. (See *Evan v. Longmont United Hospital Assn.* [68]), This affirmed the removal of staff privileges for a physician whose conduct consisted of strong hostility, an uncontrollable temper and actions which intimidated personnel of the hospital working with him in the operating room and recovery rooms of the hospital to such a degree as to disrupt the normal functioning of the operating and recovery rooms of the hospital with real and potential danger to the care of patients in the hospital.

On the other hand, what about the physician who is constantly a thorn in the side of hospital administration as a result of making complaints at staff meetings about hospital quality or management performance or the raising of concerns about the quality of care provided by other physicians or the filing of complaints with the State Board of Medical

---

[68] 629 P.2d 1100 (Colo. App. 1981)

Examiners or other outside oversight entities instead of proceeding through hospital Peer Review channels? Assume the physician to be generally disagreeable, annoying, controversial, outspoken and hypocritical of colleagues.

The conduct certainly can be described as disputative, even "disruptive", but what is being disrupted? Does the doctor's disagreeability rise to the level that it implicates the safety of patient care at the facility?

In *Miller v. Eisenhower Medical Center*,[69] the California Supreme Court said being disagreeable, annoying, controversial, outspoken, abrasive, hypercritical or personally offensive is not enough to support a loss of privileges due to "disruptive conduct". The sanction could be upheld, the court said, "only when it can be shown that the applicant's ability to work with others in the hospital setting is limited in a manner which would pose a realistic and specific threat to the quality of medical care to be afforded patients at the institution."

Basic principles of due process of law require that rules established for denial or the removal of hospital privileges not be vague or ambiguous, and that once established, they be applied effectively. [70]

---

[69] 614 P.2d 258 (Calif. 1980)
[70] See *Williams v. Kleaveland*, 534 F. Supp. 912, 917 (W.D. Mich. 1981). *Martino v. Concord Community Hospital Dist.*, 43 Cal. Rptr. 255, 260 (Calif. App. 1965) and *Kiester v. Humana Hospital Alaska et al.*, 843 P.2d 1219 (Alaska 1992).

8 Examples of Disruptive Physician Proceedings:

Some examples of conduct that could, but generally should not, give rise to a disruptive physician proceeding include:

1. Whistle blowing to outside public agencies.

2. Striving for a high level of competence or considering oneself to be right most of the time in clinical judgments.

3. Resisting a hospital administration's authority as it relates to medical concerns.

4. Expressing views disagreeable to a hospital administration.

5. Refusing to join in a hospital-sponsored venture or offering a service that competes with the hospital.

6. Requesting the hospital start a random Drug and Alcohol Testing program for hospital physicians.

7. Requesting that the hospital board replace the current hospital CEO.

8. Referring to medical staff officers as "lackeys" of the hospital administration.

Case in Point: Physician Anger Management in Wyoming

Dr. Chris Guier, M.D., who is apparently a competent and intense orthopedic surgeon, has an anger management problem. On February 24, 2011, the Wyoming Supreme Court affirmed his termination as a member of the St. John's Medical Center hospital in Jackson, Wyoming because of disruptive behavior. (See *Guier v. Teton Co. Hospital District.* [71]) In doing so the hospital skipped over the procedures in the hospital's Disruptive Physician policy and proceeded to directly terminate him under the hospital's Medical Staff By-laws.

The hospital's bylaws provided that the physician has the burden to prove that the adverse recommendation by the medical staff was without merit by a preponderance of the evidence. Dr. Guier argued that that standard was unfair and conflicted with the provisions of Wyoming's administrative procedure act. The operating room staff at the hospital had refused on three occasions, over some fourteen years, to work with Dr. Guier in the operating room.

In 2006, in a reappointment agreement, Dr. Guier agreed to a set of narrow limitations designed to control his explosive displays of anger. His conduct seems largely related to frustrations with the process of events in the operating room. "Level 10 yelling," tossing of scissors, demeaning comments and name-calling. Dr. Guier perhaps could have used some

---

[71] 248 P 3d 623(WY 2011).

Anger Management therapy. There is an interesting scene in the movie, *Anger Management*, in which Adam Sandler as patient, and Jack Nicholson as therapist, suddenly block traffic on a New York city bridge during rush hour. Nicholson grabs the car's handbrake in response to Sandler's mounting anger and requires him to go to a different place with his anger by singing "I feel pretty, oh so pretty..." Singing in the operating room may lead to other types of intervention but it is an innovative concept.

The Wyoming Supreme Court in affirming the trial court and the Medical Staff both determined that pure angry behavior was enough to terminate a competent physician's privileges, quoted the Oregon Supreme Court in *Huffaker v. Bailey*; [72]

> *Most other courts have found that the factor of an ability to work with others is reasonably related to the hospital's object of ensuring patient welfare. This conclusion seems justified for, in the modern hospital, staff members are frequently required to work together or in teams, and a member who, because of personality or otherwise, is incapable of getting along, could diversely hinder the effective treatment of patients.* [73]

A surgeon singing in the operating room may be disconcerting and probably annoying, but there has not yet been a single case reporting it to constitute disruptive conduct. Hopefully these kinds of

---

[72] 540 P 2d 1398 (Or. 1975).
[73] Op. cit. at 637.

interventions (Anger Management classes?) can develop earlier in the process.

Temper Tantrum in the O.R.

"Jumping Jelly Beans" and Surgeon's "very bad day" Lead to Summary Suspension and NPDB Report.

"Pitching a fit" in a hospital operating room can land a surgeon in the National Practitioner Data Bank. In *Leal, M.D. v. Secretary, U.S. Dept. of HHS* [74] issued on September 22, 2010, the 11th Circuit Court of Appeals affirmed the decision of the trial court upholding the determination by the Secretary of HHS that Dr. Leal's 60-day suspension for Disruptive Conduct was accurately reported and was required to be reported to the Data Bank.

When notified that there would be a delay in the start time for a urological surgery case, Dr. Leal broke a telephone, shattered the glass on a copier, shoved a metal cart into the O.R. doors causing damage, threw jelly beans down the hallway, threw a patient chart on the floor and verbally abused a nurse. In his Review Petition to the Secretary of Health and Human Services, he suggested that he had merely been clumsy; a portrayal the court was reluctant to accept from a Urological Surgeon.

---

[74] 620 F 3d 1280 (11th Cir. 2009)

The Court of Appeals obviously had some fun with this case giving it a chance to refer to Judith Viorst's book, *A Terrible, Horrible, No Good, Very Bad Day*, to describe Dr. Leal's puerile behavior leading to his suspension. Dr. Leal's objections to the Secretary's determination seemed ill-considered and petulant as well. He suggested that in order to be reportable that his behavior must have created an imminent threat to patient harm. That was a losing argument. Surgery is a team event, requiring the coordination and collaboration of physicians, technicians and nurses who need to cooperate with each other and anticipate each other's needs for the benefit of the patient. As the court noted, obnoxious behavior by a physician can lead to disruption of the ideal level of functioning of the team.

> *When a physician becomes enraged and lashes out at other members of the medical staff, patient welfare is endangered.* [75]

---

[75] Ibid at 1286.

CHAPTER 9

The Multi-State License Ricochet

The Ricochet Effect exists when a physician with multi-state licenses develops a problem with a State Board in one of state board's jurisdictions. Dr. Robert C. Gross is a physician who held licenses in Colorado, Michigan and Illinois. He was practicing in Illinois but decided to return to Michigan to practice after running into issues before the Colorado Board of Medical Examiners and its reporting him to the Data Bank, thus keeping Dr. Gross one step ahead of an Illinois report. A hospital in Colorado reported that he had failed to meet professional standards in seven surgical cases. He, in response, stated that he was being punished by the hospital for objecting to the quality of care in the facility.

Dr. Gross entered into an agreement with the Colorado Board of Medical Examiners that he would put his Colorado license on permanent "inactive" status because he was returning to Michigan anyway and the Colorado Board agreed not to pursue discipline against him. The action was reported to the National Practitioner Data Bank. The State of Illinois refused to renew his license based on the Colorado action. The Illinois Administrative Law judge found that while the action in Colorado was not formal discipline, it was "disciplinary action." The Illinois Court of Appeals Agreed in *Robert C. Gross, v. The*

Department of Financial and Professional Regulation.[76]

> *Although we find that the Colorado Board did not impose discipline on Dr. Gross after a hearing, we hold that the Department did not commit clear error when it concluded that the Colorado Board had taken "disciplinary action" against Dr. Gross's license. The Department's finding justified the decision to place Dr. Gross's Illinois license in "Refuse to Renew" status. Accordingly, we affirm the judgment of the trial court and the Department.*[77]

In other words, the non-discipline in Colorado was discipline in Illinois and Dr. Gross lost his license to practice there.

The State of Michigan, even though aware of the Colorado action continued to allow Dr. Gross to practice in Michigan. The question now is whether Michigan will continue to do so, now that Illinois has take disciplinary action against him based upon the non-disciplinary action in Colorado, which is also reportable to the Data Bank and which in turn may cause Colorado to reopen its discipline. So it goes.

---

[76]

http://www.state.il.us/court/Opinions/AppellateCourt/2011/1stDistrict/November/1103101.pdf

[77] Id.

CHAPTER 10

Non-Peer Review: Liability Outside the Scope of Peer Review

Review of Dr. Ayadeji O. Bakare, M.D.

A Federal District Court for the Middle District of Pennsylvania dismissed multiple claims against Pinnacle Health Hospitals, Inc. (Pinnacle) and a number of physicians, which arose out of the Peer Review of Dr. Ayadeji O. Bakare, M.D., but permitted a defamation action against Dr. Barry B. Moore, M.D. and his employer, Pinnacle to proceed.

In *Bakare, M.D. v. Pinnacle Health Hospitals, Inc.* et al.,[78] Dr. Bakare, a board-certified OB/Gyn physician, sought recovery of damages based upon claims of anti-trust violations, breach of contract, interference and defamation arising out of his precautionary suspension from the Pinnacle medical staff and an adverse recommendation from the Medical Executive Committee that his medical staff privileges be revoked. Pinnacle lifted Dr. Bakare's suspension shortly after it was imposed following an agreement worked out between the parties to limit the scope of Dr. Bakare's practice pending the investigation. The adverse recommendation as to his privileges was reinforced by an independent outside review by a

---

[78] Civil Action 1:03-cv-1098 (Aug. 24, 2006)

physician recommended by the Academy of Obstetrics and Gynecology (ACOG).

Dr. Bakare requested and received a "fair hearing" before Pinnacle's Fair Hearing Committee (FHC). The FHC met fifteen times over four months, listened to thirty hours of testimony and deliberated over four hours. The FHC concluded that the adverse action of the MEC was in error. and that the MEC received misinformation concerning the cases. The FHC found that the MEC acted "reasonably and responsibly" based on the information presented to it, but that the information was wrong. The MEC accepted the FHC findings and conclusions and reversed its adverse recommendation.

The court determined that immunity under HCQIA applied and that Dr. Bakare couldn't demonstrate by a preponderance of the evidence that the MEC action was not undertaken "in the reasonable belief that the action was in furtherance of quality healthcare," (after a reasonable effort to obtain the facts), or that there was any defect in the nature and hearing procedures.

Dr. Bakare himself testified that if he had heard the evidence presented to the MEC, he would have agreed with the MEC's conclusion.

The court also dismissed Dr. Bakare's antitrust claims because of lack of evidence and the failure of Dr. Bakare to establish antitrust damages so as to provide him standing to bring his case (i.e., Dr. Bakare could not demonstrate that his loss advanced the anti-competitive agenda of the defendants.) Then the court addressed a discussion between the defendant Dr. Moore and a number of nurses in the operating room lounge shortly following Dr. Bakare's precautionary suspension.

Dr. Moore apparently advised the nurses that he was tired because he had been working on an investigating Executive Committee looking into the quality of care by Dr. Bakare. Dr. Moore allegedly told the nurses that Dr. Bakare was being investigated for the poor quality of his care for his OB/Gyn patients away from the operating room. Although there is a dispute as to what Dr. Moore actually said, the court said that there was sufficient evidence for a reasonable jury to conclude that Dr. Moore told the nurses that Dr. Bakare provided bad care and that the statement by Dr. Moore was false. The court denied the motion to dismiss the Defamation Claim against Dr. Moore.

The court also denied Pinnacle's Motion to Dismiss on the Defamation Claim because Dr. Bakare's claim against it was based on Vicarious Liability for the conduct of Dr. Moore, who was an employee of Pinnacle, acting within the scope of his employment. Since Dr. Moore's discussion with the nurses occurred outside of the Peer Review process, there was no immunity protection.

This result is yet another reason why Peer Review proceedings should be isolated from hospital "chit chat" and that confidentiality be strictly enforced. The immunity tent for Peer Review is large, but it only covers genuine Peer Review activity.

The Curious Case of Dr. John Doe

MONTANA SUPREME COURT AFFIRMS INJUNCTION AGAINST HOSPITAL SUSPENSION OF PHYSICIAN WHO DENIED IT ACCESS TO HIS FAMILY'S PRIVATE MEDICAL RECORDS.

The Montana Supreme Court affirmed the issuance of a preliminary injunction restraining Community Medical Center, a hospital in Missoula, Montana, for suspending the medical staff privileges of a hospitalist whose only offense was to refuse to grant unrestricted access to his family's medical records to a hospital subcommittee outside of the Peer Review system. The physician designated as "Dr. Doe," in the case of *John Doe, M.D. v. Community Medical Center, Inc.,* [79] asserted that that Community Medical Center (CMC) breached the terms of its contract with him embodied in CMC's medical staff bylaws and policies by summarily suspending his privileges with no demonstration of "a substantial likelihood of imminent impairment of the health or safety of any patient, prospective patient, employee or other person present in the medical center" – the sole bylaw designated basis for summary suspension at CMC.

Dr. John Doe's children had been diagnosed earlier with a rare, life-threatening condition involving Panhypopituitarism. During 2007 and 2008, Dr. Doe ordered numerous outpatient laboratory tests and imaging studies for himself, his wife and his children.

---

[79] 221 P 3d 651 (MT 2009).

CMC confronted Dr. Doe, expressing concern that such testing might constitute unethical medical treatment of his family members. Dr. Jan Hiller, the Chief of the Medical Staff of CMC, asked for an investigation by the Medical/Allied Health Staff Assistance Committee, a committee organized primarily for dealing with serious behavioral issues like drug or alcohol addiction and not a designated "Peer Review" committee.

The committee obtained outpatient medical records of Dr. Doe and his family from CMC and from another hospital, St. Patrick's Hospital, without Dr. Doe's knowledge or consent. The committee asked Dr. Doe to disclose the names of all physicians treating each member of his family and to authorize direct access to them by the committee. When Dr. Doe refused to comply at a committee meeting, Dr. Hiller suspended him on the grounds that:

> *[H]is demeanor and refusal or inability to coherently answer routine and legitimate questions regarding the volume and nature of the tests caused me to have serious and legitimate concerns regarding his mental health and ability to exercise good judgment.* [80]

"Good judgment" being in the eye of the superior beholder, the Supreme Court sided with the trial court in favor of Dr. Doe. The very crux of Dr. Doe's complaint in the district court was the complete absence of any evidence or even suggestion by the Medical Examining Committee that Dr. Doe's conduct

---

[80] Ibid at 380.

had placed the health or safety of any patient or other person in the medical center in jeopardy. Therefore, he alleged that there were no facts justifying suspension nor was there a legal basis for summarily suspending his privileges. This being so, the suspension and ensuing proposed Peer Review were outside the parameters of the bylaws, and as such constituted a Breach of Contract.

The court rejected CMC's arguments that Dr. Doe was required to first exhaust his administrative remedies before going to court, that the state law was implicitly pre-empted by the Healthcare Quality Improvement Act of 1986, and that the injunction was an unwarranted interference with the police powers and duties of the Montana Board of Medical Examiners. It also rejected CMC's argument that any harm to Dr. Doe's reputation from CMC's federally-required report of any suspension lasting more than thirty days to the National Practitioner Data Bank could be dispelled by a later filing of a voiding report in the event Dr. Doe did prevail in a post-suspension hearing ("[T]he fact is that a ringing bell cannot be unrung.").[81]

The court noted that there was credible testimony in the transcript that Dr. Doe is an "excellent physician," who exhibited no behavior that would suggest that he was incapable, incompetent, or not qualified" to practice as a hospitalist at CMC and that CMC demonstrated no specific behavioral issue other than his refusal to provide private medical information regarding his children and his refusal to sign a blanket waiver of confidentiality. While acknowledging the

---

[81] Ibid at 391

value and importance of the Peer Review process, the court refused to preclude a physician from access to the courts of the state where the process goes awry.

> *Notwithstanding the validity and propriety of Peer Review as a process whereby a physician who endangers patients or other persons within the Medical Center can be immediately reviewed by his peers, we cannot preclude a physician from gaining access to the courts to remedy an ostensible breach of contract.* [82]

It appears after all, that even doctors and their families have protection at law to support their right to medical privacy, where it does not directly impinge upon the legitimate interests of hospitals, medical staffs and their patients.

---

[82] Ibid at 389.

Physician Email Rant Provides Liability Evidence

In *Allison Moon v. Michigan Reproductive and IVF Center, P.C. and Grand Rapids Fertility and IVF, P.C.* ,[83] the Michigan Court of Appeals entered an unpublished, per curium decision reversing a trial court dismissal of a state civil rights suit for discrimination based on marital status when the defendant refused to treat the patient with in vitro fertilization because she was a single woman.

Michigan's Elliott-Larsen Civil Rights Act, known as ELCRA, prohibits discrimination by "a place of public accommodation" based on marital status. Dr. Daly from the Grand Rapids facility sent plaintiff an impassioned, ranting email refusing to provide IVF treatment to a single patient because of fears of lawyers imposing liability on him (as in a Boston case), for the costs of raising a fatherless child until maturity. This is perhaps an abject lesson to all professionals about being careful with Internet communications.

The court, in its decision, stated;

> *Moon proffered direct evidence of potential discrimination from the e-mail messages she received from Dr. Daly, indicating that GRFI does not provide IVF treatment to single women. Dr. Daly's statement, "[u]ntil I feel there is*

---

[83] LC No-004732 CZ (Mich. App. September 29, 2011)

> *adequate law I will not be providing*
> *insemination services to single*
> *individuals," tends to establish "that*
> *unlawful discrimination was at least a*
> *motivating factor" in Dr. Daly's decision*
> *to deny Moon IVF services.* [84]

Dr. Daly presumably now has something closer to home to fuel his anger.

---

[84] 2011 WL 3795599 (8/29/11)

Female Neurosurgeon's $2.9M Harassment Claim

The 1st Circuit Court of Appeals affirmed a Harassment Judgment brought by a female neurosurgeon against a Boston hospital affiliated with the Harvard Healthcare system in the amount of $2.9 million. In the case of *Tuli v. Brigham & Woman's Hospital*, [85] the 1st Circuit Court of Appeals affirmed the judgment of the trial court in favor of Dr. Tuli. The court affirmed that Dr. Arthur Day and Dr. Kim Dong created a hostile work environment by making comments about Dr. Tuli that were blatantly sexist and humiliating. Dr. Tuli complained to the hospital's Chief Medical Officer, without receiving any remedy.

The court also found that the jury could reasonably have found that Dr. Day, as Residency Director and Department Vice-chairman, retaliated against her for her complaints to the hospital by misleading the Hospital Credentials Committee, which required Dr. Tuli to receive outside counseling in order to obtain a continuation of her privileges. Allegations of mental illness are frequent weapons used in a Sham Peer Review process. Even though wrapped in the friendly construct of "counseling," the recommendation could reasonably be considered as sufficiently onerous and to be an "adverse action" prompted by a retaliatory motive.

Dr. Day apparently played the female hormone card. He told the Hospital Credentials Committee that Dr. Tuli experienced "mood swings" and that surgical

---

[85] 719 N.W.2d 1 (Mich. 2006)No 08-2006,(8/29/11)

support staff did not want to work with her as a result. He suggested she undergo Anger Management treatment without mentioning to the committee the allegations she raised against him.

The Circuit Court held that the "accumulated effect of incidents of humiliating, offensive comments directed at women and work-sabotaging pranks, taken together, can constitute a hostile work environment."

The fact that Dr. Day presented this information in the re-credentialing process without disclosing Dr. Tuli's complaints against him was strong evidence of malicious and retaliatory behavior.

The Reluctance of Court Intervention

Michigan Supreme Court Jettisons Judicial Non-Intervention Doctrine in Review of Private Hospital Staffing Decisions.

Judges have long been reluctant to intervene in private hospital staffing decisions. They are frequently uncomfortable in second-guessing hospital decisions regarding the qualifications and competency of physicians. In the case of public hospitals they have had little choice. Public facilities are public actors and staffing decisions raise constitutional and civil rights issues. In June of 2006, the Michigan Supreme Court specifically rejected the Judicial Non-intervention Doctrine in private hospital disputes previously adopted by the Michigan Court of Appeals in a line of cases. In *Feyz, M.D. v. Mercy Memorial Hospital et al.*,[86] the court determined that the judicially created "Doctrine of Non-intervention" was at odds with the Michigan Peer Review immunity statute.

The case arose out of a dispute in the hospital over nursing orders for patient intake. The plaintiff, Dr. Feyz, insisted that hospital nurses use his special standing orders for patient intake rather than the one adopted by the hospital. Dr. Feyz wanted the nurses to obtain very specific information from patients about their prescription drug use. The defendants directed the nurses to ignore Dr. Feyz's instructions. Dr. Feyz created "incident reports" concerning several nurses who refused to follow his instructions. He also made

---

[86] 719 N.W.2d 1 (Mich. 2006)

chart notes that his instructions were designed to prevent serious past medication errors. Dr. Feyz refused to comply with hospital policy that physicians sign transcriptions of their verbal orders.

The hospital commenced a Peer Review investigation of Dr. Feyz for his failure to complete medical records and ordered him to undergo a psychiatric evaluation. Dr. Feyz said he discontinued signing the orders when the hospital gave him the use of a pharmacy consult service. When the hospital withdrew the service, Dr. Feyz resumed the placement of his specialized orders. The hospital placed Dr. Feyz on indefinite probation and restricted him from further use of his specialized orders. Dr. Feyz brought suit under the Persons with Disabilities Civil Rights Act, the Americans with Disabilities Act, the Rehabilitation Act of 1973, 42 U.S.C. § 1983 and § 1985, invasion of privacy, breach of fiduciary and public duties and breach of contract.

The trial court dismissed all of the claims because of immunity under the Michigan Peer Review Statute, [87] The Michigan Court of Appeals reversed the trial court in part by reinstating the civil rights claims, holding that the alleged civil rights claim was not within the scope of Peer Review and that the violation alleged was "malicious"

On further appeal, the Michigan Supreme Court rejected the "Non-Intervention" Doctrine outright because the Michigan legislature did not provide Peer

---

[87] MCL. 331.531

Review immunity for hospitals under the Peer Review Statute indicating a legislative rejection of non-intervention. Secondly, the court rejected the foundational concern that courts are not qualified to review such cases. ("This claim overlooks the reality that courts routinely review complex claims of all kinds.")

The court went on to adopt a defamation definition of "malice", which is the key to exception from Peer Review immunity – that is, actual knowledge of falsity or reckless disregard of falsity.

> *[M]aking unfavorable evaluations, determinations and recommendations based on negative information the Peer Review entity knows to be false would satisfy the malice standard...*

> *The defamation definition of "malice" promotes the goals of Peer Review because Peer Review participants are not protected if they are not performing evaluations with a focus on improving healthcare, but rather on the basis of false extraneous factors unrelated to patient care.*[88]

A Defamation Action now also appears to be one of the vehicles of choice for challenging Peer Review actions by private hospitals in the State of Michigan. Dr. Feyz will apparently have his day in court to show

---

[88] Op. cit. at 13.

that he was not being "disruptive" in demanding that more extensive prescription drug information be obtained by nurses, contrary to hospital policy.

CHAPTER 11

National Practitioner "Defamation" Bank? and Disruptive Practitioners

About the National Practitioner Data Bank

The National Practitioner Data Bank ("NPDB") [89] was a creation of Congress pursuant to HCQIA, which directed the Secretary of Health and Human Services to set up the NPDB as a mandatory repository of information regarding:

a. Malpractice suits and settlements

b. Competence based disciplinary actions undertaken against healthcare practitioners

c. State licensure actions affecting healthcare practitioners.

The idea was to provide a central, national depository of negative information about the competence and professional performance of credentialed healthcare physicians.

Congress was concerned that physicians in particular, who were disciplined in one state or arena could freely move to another state or locality and start anew despite a history of bad professional performance.
In many cases the NPDB, as currently operated, does more harm than good and serves as an instrument

---

[89] See 42 U.S.C. § 1101 et seq.

capable of falsely destroying the reputations and careers of health case practitioners.

HCQIA requires all hospitals in the U.S. to undertake an NPDB search for each physician on its medical staff at least every two years and at the time of an initial grant of hospital privileges to a physician.

A negative report from the NPDB raises a plethora of legal and practical issues for a hospital, which will likely, at a minimum, precipitate an investigation which will delay or impede the availability of medical staff privileges to the physician applicant.

Information that must be reported to the NPDB comes from three sources:

(1) Malpractice Judgments and Settlements (no matter how small) must be reported by insurance companies.

(2) Disciplinary actions by hospitals and professional societies that affect a practitioner's privilege or membership and implicate the practitioner's competence or professional activities.

(3) State licensing boards must report restrictions composed on a practitioner's license to practice.

The NPDB was set up to be self-funding, financed by all of the mandatory and discretionary user fees paid by hospitals and practitioners for access to the information, if any, in the Data Bank. The work of the NPDB is largely automated and many, if not most, of the reporting is never reviewed by human eyes at the NPDB.

Once filed, it is near impossible to effectively rebut information and extremely difficult to effect corrections. Further, there is no time limit to the information as the scarlet letter **I** ("I" for incompetent) lasts forever.

Eighty percent of the adverse reports to the Data Bank are malpractice reports of settlements with insurance companies.

Any physician named in a malpractice suit, no matter how frivolous the case or how low the settlement amount is, must be reported to the NPDB if a payment is made on his behalf to settle the lawsuit.

There are now approximately 250,000 physicians listed in the Data Bank.

NPDB reports rarely carry information as to whether the settlement involved an evaluation of failure to meet the standards of practice. Occasionally the same incident is reported twice leaving the impression that more settlements are involved than is actually the case.

HCQIA does provide a caveat to Data Bank reviewers:

Interpretation of Information:

> *In interpreting reported under this part of payment is settlement of a medical practice action or claim shall not be construed as creating a presumption that malpractice has occurred.* [90]

No presumption of malpractice? Pretty cold comfort, that is. As a physician "you are in the Data Bank now," or "*banked*," as they say, and unless you have a contractual provision in your insurance policy providing for the right to refuse consent to the report there is scant recourse.

The courts have generally not been sympathetic when practitioners attempt to sue their insurance companies or attorneys for failing to obtain their consent for a settlement. [90]

In November 2000, the United States General Accounting Office (GAO) issued a report sharply critical of the NPDB. [91] The GAO reported that more than 95% of the malpractice reports did not mention

---

[90] See *Miller v. Sloan, Listrom, Eisenbarth, Sloan & Glassmar, et al.*, 1999 WL 23085, 978 P.2d 922 (Kansas 1999) (finding that plaintiff physician suffered no apparent damages and that insurance contract left discretion to settle exclusively in the insurance company). *Shuster v. South Broward Hospital Dist.*, 591 So.2d 174 (Fla. 1992) (insurer had broad discretion as to when and how to settle a case). *Bleday v. OUM Group*, 645 A.2d 1358 (1994) (bad faith settlement of malpractice insurance claim only available in limited circumstances as when insurer indiscriminately settles with one or more of the parties for full amount of policy exposing insured to an excess judgment from other parties).
[91] GAO-01-130)

whether the standard of patient care had been considered when the claim was resolved, which of course opens the assumption that they all were.

Reports are submitted electronically and are not manually screened before accepted by the NPDB, and NPDB staff does not routinely review the narrative information for completeness or propriety for filing. Clinical privilege restriction reports also failed the GAO review.

The GAO found coding errors in one third of the reports it examined, leading to the concern that those purchasing copies of the NPDB public use file might be misled about the severity of disciplinary actions taken against practitioners.

Data Bank officials rely on practitioner notification and dispute resolution proceedings to insure the accuracy of reports, but the GAO noted that the controls did not prevent inaccurate information from remaining in the Data Bank once it is reported.

It is notoriously difficult to obtain corrections in the Data Bank. The GAO report noted a case, in which a hospital reported discipline of a physician for poor record keeping. The doctor disputed the report based on the fact that there was no restriction on his clinical privileges. The hospital attempted to correct the information by requesting a cancellation of the report, but incorrectly coded the action as a state license revocation. The report noted both the initial incorrect report and the report on license revocation were still in the Data Bank a year later. [92] As of 2012, the Data Bank has just completed reports that were filed in 2008.

Recent revelations regarding federal agencies that employ physicians have not been reporting malpractice and other incidents to the state banks because of general fairness concerns underscore the flaws of the Data Bank.

Inaccurate Data Bank reports frequently submitted by bureaucrats to undiscerning Data Bank computers can destroy or injure medical careers and can require enormous expense in attorney fees and costs to obtain corrections.

If the Data Bank is to continue, the government should develop procedures for routinely checking the accuracy and completeness of information reported to it and for obtaining corrections from reporters, as recommended by the GAO. This should include an administrative procedure for resolving disputes more effectively and inexpensively. A procedure is also needed for expunging of a record based on a showing that a report is no longer relevant to the abilities or capacities of a physician.

Forever is a long time to wear a scarlet letter.

---

[92] GAO Report at 25.

The National Practitioner Data Bank's Duty to Investigate Disputed Reports.

Under HCQIA, hospitals, state medical practice boards and other entities have duties to report certain actions and suspensions of physicians, dentists and certain other practitioners to the specially created NPDB.

Hospitals are required by HCQIA to inquire of the Data Bank every two years concerning doctors and dentists on their medical staffs who are seeking the renewal of their hospital privileges.

A physician or dentist who is reported to the Data Bank may well find his career at an end because of the reluctance of hospitals to grant privileges to a professional with documented "quality" or "competence" problems or issues.

Not infrequently, providers are "coerced" into resigning from a medical staff or independently seek to avoid a Data Bank report by resigning from the Medical Staff.

Unfortunately, resignation during a pending hospital investigation or to avoid a hospital investigation also triggers a reportable event.

Under the rules regarding disputes concerning reported events, [93] a physician or dentist may submit a notice to the Secretary of HHS of the existence of a dispute with the report within 60 days of the mailing of the original notice of the report by the Secretary.

In the case of *Simpkins v. Donna E. Shallala*, [94] the District of Columbia U.S. District Court ruled that the Secretary had a duty to investigate the facts of the dispute to determine whether the reporting obligation was properly triggered. The Secretary could not simply get by with indicating that a dispute existed as to the facts.

The court in Simpkins found that Dr. Simpkins did in fact resign from the medical staff, but that he did not resign "while under investigation" concerning the quality of his care. The court held that a negative review by Dr. Simpkins' supervisor did not constitute the type of formal "entity" investigation required to implicate the reporting requirement.

> *Thus the text of the relevant statute and regulation signify that formal action by the hospital, as an organization, triggers [HCQIA's] reporting provisions, not individual action.* [95]

The court cited NPDB's own guidebook for the proposition that the reporting hospital must provide

---

[93] 45 CFR 60.14
[94] 999 F. Supp. 106 (D. D.C. 1998)
[95] Ibid at 114.

contemporaneous evidence to the NPDB of an ongoing investigation at the time of the surrender of privileges.

The court ordered that Dr. Simpkins, name be removed from the NPDB where he was identified as having resigned his clinical privileges while under investigation. The court held that because the investigation conducted by the hospital did not qualify as an investigation to trigger the reporting requirements under HCQIA, in that the hospital did not follow its bylaws.

Also, the "review" of Dr. Simpkins did not follow the hospital's procedure. The hospital provided no documentation to HHS that a complaint of any kind was ever submitted to its Medical Director. As a result, the specified investigatory procedures mandated by the hospital's bylaws were never initiated.

Dr. Simpkins received no complaint nor was "an investigating committee" appointed as required by the hospital bylaws. These deviations from the by-laws were not minor but rather fundamental in nature and indicate that these actions cannot be reasonably found to constitute an investigation by the hospital.

Getting Out of the National Practitioner Data Bank:

Once a physician or other healthcare provider is reported to the National Practitioner Data Bank, he or she is normally there for life. It is extremely difficult to get out. Some physicians have remarked that it is like having a "record," in the criminal context which can result in the denial of hospital privileges, denial of jobs and potentially the destruction of careers.

All hospitals are required to access the Data Bank reports on physicians every two years during hospital privileges re-certifications. State disciplinary actions are required to be reported as well as malpractice insurance payments (no matter the amount). Peer Review discipline is also reportable, although there are some limited exceptions.

A hospital must report any physician or other practitioner who resigns while under "investigation" in order to avoid disciplinary action. The term "investigation" is not defined in either HCQIA, the implementing statute or in any ensuring regulations.

In *John Doe v. Michael Leavitt,* [96] the U.S. 1st Circuit Court of Appeals, affirmed a Maine U.S. District Court holding that the term "investigation" was to be broadly construed to include not only fact finding, but also ongoing activity of the healthcare entity through due process to final action or the formal close of the proceedings. In Doe, a physician who resigned his

---

[96] 552 F 3d 75,(Ist Cir. ,2009.

privileges rather than undergo regular proctoring and psychological evaluations, was required to be reported to the Data Bank. The physician argued that the "investigation" definition was limited to the fact-finding process.

The court agreed with the District Court and the Secretary of Health and Human Services that the purpose of the reporting requirement was essential to plug a loophole for physicians resigning in lieu of discipline and that to limit the definition of investigation would contradict the purpose of the statute.

There is perhaps an irony here that the discipline recommended, as described by the court, may not have been sufficiently onerous under the reporting guidelines so as to require reporting to the Data Bank if it had been accepted.

The next question will obviously be what happens if the physician enters an agreement with the hospital to resign, but only after termination of proceedings. Probably the same result.

In *Costa, M.D. v. Leavitt,* [97] a doctor successfully pried open the lid on the Data Bank by establishing that the record did not reflect that he was "under investigation" when he resigned his privileges. Dr. Costa had had a long and hostile relationship with the hospital administrator and the hospital board and appeared to be somewhat of a gadfly around Gothenburg Memorial Hospital. He challenged the competency of the hospital administrator, who he

---

[97] 2006 U.S. Dist. Lexis 51675,

described as a "tin horn". He derided the board for failing to properly supervise the administrator and expressed general disdain for both. The record reflected that the hospital's denial of Dr. Costa's request for renewal of his privileges just before he resigned was a result of his disdain and not part of a professional review action.

The hospital administrator first reported Dr. Costa to the Data Bank suggesting that he was under investigation by the State of Nebraska, which was a false statement. He later recanted that statement but then suggested that there was an ongoing review related to Dr. Costa's obstetric cases and his alleged inadequate supervision of a physician's assistant.

Although there was mention of those issues in meetings, there was no apparent contemporary documentation of a formal investigation commenced under the bylaws of the hospital.

The court went on to find that the narrative description required in the report to the Data Bank was inadequate in that it only generally reported that the resignation occurred while under investigation related to professional competence and did not provide specifics. While noting that a great deal of specificity is not required, it does require sufficient specificity to enable a knowledgeable observer to determine clearly the circumstances of the action or surrender. [98]

Escape is difficult, but not impossible, if the facts are right. Getting out of the NPDB is perhaps equivalent to escaping from Alcatraz – a near impossible feat.

---

[98] See NPDB Guidebook F-7.

Yet there are those who have accomplished it. The easiest way of course is to convince the hospital or other reporting entity that the report was improvidently submitted and that it should be retracted and withdrawn which they are able to do by filing additional documentation with the National Practitioner Data Bank. The other option is to convince the Secretary of HHS that based on the administrative record, the submission was in error and not reportable under the criteria for reporting set out in the NPDB guidebook.

If the Secretary of Health and Human Services persists in affirming the appropriateness of the report, the only remaining recourse is the filing of a judicial review action in a federal court under the federal Administrative Procedure Act, 5 U.S.C. §701 et seq., where you must establish that the decision by the Secretary was "arbitrary and capricious."

One of the most contentions areas of Data Bank reporting is the obligation to report a physician who resigns or withdraws an application for privileges in order to avoid a Peer Review "investigation" or discipline.

128

CHAPTER 12

Insurance Policies: Consent to Settlement

As more physicians elect to join larger physician groups and hospitals as employed physicians, many are finding to their surprise that the Professional Liability policies provided to them by their employers fail to include the right on the part of the physician to approve any settlement.

It is not unheard of for insurance companies to settle a case without the knowledge, consent or approval of their insured. This can have a significant impact on the future and career of a physician because all malpractice must be reported to the National Practitioner Data Bank and all hospitals are required to access NPDB each time a physician is re-credentialed. Having a NPDB report is treated by some potential employers and credentialing hospitals as equivalent to "having a record."

Insurance policies that contain the Right to Object to a malpractice settlement tend to cost more than those without the clause. The incentive on the part of a hospital employer may well be to obtain the cheaper policy as well as to exclude the possibility of the physician objecting to a settlement that would be in the best interests of the hospital.

It is almost inevitable that a hospital employer will be sued along with its employee physician on any malpractice lawsuit. Not infrequently those suits also name everybody who had any contact with the plaintiff, no matter how slight or remote. An unallocated global settlement that releases all the physicians involved, even those who had no real likelihood of exposure, nevertheless must be reported to the NPDB, which of course hardly seems fair.

In 2005, in the case of *Webb v. Witt*,[99] the Appellate Division of the Superior Court of New Jersey upheld the denial of a motion by one of the defendant physicians sued by a minor injured at birth, to herself sue her own hospital employer and insurance company to allocate a global settlement among the participants in a settlement.

The court held that absent an express provision granting such a right in the contract of insurance, the physician had no right to object to a settlement or to an adjudication hearing.

> *We hold that such a physician or practitioner has no right to object to the settlement nor to demand an apportionment of his or her responsibility before the settlement is reported to either the National Practitioner Data Bank or the New Jersey Division of Consumer Affairs.* [100]

---

[99] 876 A. 2d 858 (App. Div. 2005)
[100] Ibid at 860.

Any physician joining a hospital or group practice should ask for and pay attention to the provisions of the group or hospital insurance coverage policy to negotiate or ensure that the there is a right to approval settlements in the policy coverage.

It is also essential to pay attention to the renewals or replacement of policies. Otherwise, a physician's reputation can be lodged in the Data Bank without fault or recourse for the physician.

In *Teague, M.D. v. St Paul Fire and Marine Insurance Company, et al.,* [101] Dr. Teague sued his insurance company for settling his claim without notifying him.

The court, noting that there is always a conflict between the desire of a defendant to vindicate himself and the insurance company's desire to minimize the cost of litigation and to avoid the risk of loss, held that there was no conflict between Dr. Teague's insurance company and his attorneys, where Dr. Teague had contracted away his right of consent to settlement.

> *Defendants who settle face an uphill battle in convincing others, including members of the of the interested public or the media that they were completely innocent of the charges... These are the ordinary consequences of settlement. A party purchasing a*

---

[101] 10 So.3d 806 (La. App. 4/7/09)

> *liability insurance policy containing the duty to defend language at issue here agrees to accept the insurer's view concerning the point at which the benefits of settlement exceed the risk of continuing litigation. The alternative is to negotiate-and pay for-a policy with a consent provisions.* [102]

Several reported cases exist dealing with an insurance company's discretion in allocating settlement responsibility so as to implicate Data Bank reporting.

In *Melendez v. The Hospital For Joint Diseases Orthopedic Institute, et al.* [103] a hospital-employed surgeon moved for an order modifying the proposed settlement of a malpractice lawsuit to reflect no payment made on his behalf. The court held that absent any employment contract provision giving surgeon the right to object to the proposed settlement, the potential impact of the report on the surgeon's career did not entitle the surgeon to blanket insulation from the collateral effects of the settlement.

In *John Doe, M.D. v. South Carolina Medical Malpractice Liability Joint Underwriting Association*, [104] the physician brought a Bad Faith claim against the underwriting association for allocating all of the settlement claim against him, when there were other defendants.

---

[102] Ibid at 820
[103] 575 N.Y.S. 2d 636 (NY Super. 1991)
[104] (S.C. 2001)

He didn't contest that he was at fault; he only claimed that he was not solely at fault. The court held that the evidence did not show bad faith in the allocation and dismissed the action. [105]

Physicians would be well served by a careful examination and understanding of their professional liability policies and should explore the price differential that would give the physician, rather than the insurance company, final control over the settlement decision.

---

[105] See also, *Babic, M.D. v. Physician's Protective Defense Fund*, 738 So. 2d 442 (Fla. App. 1999)(insurer immune on claim that it inaccurately reported allocation of liability in the settlement of malpractice litigation).

134

CHAPTER 13

Eight Reforms to Medical Peer Review

The fundamental problem with medical Peer Review today is that there are large segments of medical practice that are more art than science and that all professionals are human beings and occasionally make mistakes.

The system of Peer Review provided under the HealthCare Quality Improvement Act of 1986 ("HCQIA") sets up an intensely adversarial system in which those privileged to review their peers are not accountable for bias, bad faith, or malice if there is any colorable justification for complaint about the judgment or quality of care provided by the reviewed physician. Further, the results can destroy a Peer Reviewed physician who may end up with a "record" in the National Practitioner Data Bank.

The so-called "objective," "reasonable belief," HCQIA standard of review in granting immunity, as interpreted by the courts, immunizes a Peer Reviewer no matter how transparently malicious or biased he or she may be, if there is any arguably factual basis supporting the purported existence of a "reasonable belief" that the Peer Review action against a physician is in furtherance of quality patient care.

In an editorial championing absolute immunity for Peer Reviewers the American Medical News stated that physicians were too ethical and professional to engage in Sham Peer Review.

> *It is not only that physicians are expected to personally embrace the professional and ethical standards that would make such an action untenable. Discovery of such a dishonest act would seriously jeopardize their standing among colleagues and in the institutions where they practice.* [106]

The author is "not in Kansas anymore." Perhaps he or she missed an important part of reality education relating to institutional politics.

Professional politicians are perhaps more "objective." John Emerich Edward Dalberg Acton a.k.a. "Lord Acton," famously wrote in the late 19th Century in England that "Power tends to corrupt and absolute power corrupts absolutely." William Pitt, the elder and formidable British Prime Minister, no stranger to political reality and human nature, stated, "Unlimited power is apt to corrupt the minds of those who possess it."

A number of reforms could improve the system of Peer Review and help limit the cannibalistic tendencies in play.

Here are eight.

---

[106] "Peer Review: The Case For Absolute Immunity," AMNEWS, March 15, 2004. See
http://www.ama.assn.org/amednews/2004/03/15/edsa0315.htm

Improving Peer Reviews:

1. Remove the so-called "objective" Standard of Immunity to permit sanctions for bad faith in Peer Review.

2. Eliminate the "catch all" provision in the due process requirements set forth in HCQIA that gives and takes away the protections provided therein by exculpating processes that fail to follow the statute by permitting some undefined minimal level of due process that the courts have been quick to validate.

3. Make all Peer Review panels truly independent by permitting those affected, at their cost, to opt for a hearing by a standing independent body of physicians in his or her own specialty.

4. Make malpractice settlements reportable to the National Practitioner Data Bank only where there is some minimal threshold level of payment made so as to eliminate reporting for Nuisance Value Settlements by insurance companies.

5. Permit physicians whose insurance contracts do not provide for Consent to Settlement to submit the malpractice claim for review to an independent body of physicians to determine whether the physician's conduct failed to meet the

standard of care before reporting to the Data Bank.

6. Provide for the one time option of retraining and recertification of physicians by a university or specialty certification organization in lieu of a report to the National Practitioner Data Bank to place a greater premium and emphasis on rehabilitation rather than on sanctioning and branding.

7. Eliminate immunity for the sanctioning of physicians for "disagreeable" conduct that is based upon a legitimate, bona fide complaint or concern by the physician over the quality of care or other practices in a hospital, where the conduct of the physician is not shown to rise to the level of immediate, rather than theoretical risk of disruption and patient harm.

8. Require a specific time frame for the Secretary of HH&S to act on objections by physicians to the propriety of filings with the National Practitioner Data Bank, so as to make the NPDB process meaningful and useful.

Given the cost, time and effort that goes into the production of a medical professional, his or her career should not be so lightly shielded from the whim, malice and/or opportunism of others in a profession that sometimes eats its young.

Reader's Comment on "Eight Reforms To Medical Peer Review Post." *01/01/2012*

[Ed. note] Below is a thoughtful comment submitted by a person associated with the NPDB with a contrary view:

Until my retirement three years ago I was Associate Director for Research and Disputes for HRSA's National Practitioner Data Bank. For over 10 years I read every Secretarial Review request, assigned every case to staff reviewers, and approved every decision before forwarding it for final approval and signature by the Director. In other words, I have great familiarity with this matter.

Before turning to the eight suggestions, I must take issue with the implication that a report to the NPDB can destroy a career. It is the underlying actions that hurt careers, not reports to the Data Bank. Applications for licensure, privileges, etc., require physicians to disclose more than is required to be reported to the Data Bank. For example, the Data Bank does not require reporting of pending cases; applications do. Honest physicians have nothing to fear from Data Bank reports; they have to disclose the same information regardless of the Data Bank.

It also should be noted that there are thousands of physicians with multiple reports in the Data Bank who continue to practice and, often, to have even more actions taken against them and reported. If the Data Bank ended careers, physicians would not continue to have action after action taken against them.

Turning to the eight suggested reforms for Peer Review:

1. Based on my experience with reviewing Secretarial Review cases, I would agree that there are some bad faith Peer Review actions, but I think they are relatively uncommon. Under the law Secretarial Review is not a forum for re-trying Peer Review cases; the Secretary is not the "Supreme Court" of Peer Review. And I suspect most physicians would not want that. The government should not substitute its judgment for that of Peer Reviewers. This, of course, made it impossible for us in Secretarial Review to remove reports from the Data Bank, let alone reverse the underlying actions, when we believed there had been bad faith but the record supported the accuracy of the report in terms of the action taken and the reasons in the record for the action. But in such circumstance we typically raised some very pointed questions with reporting institutions, and this often resulted in a much more satisfactory result for the physician. In other instances the Secretary added comments to reports noting concerns. I should also point out that about 20 percent of Secretarial Review cases result in an outcome in favor of the complaining physician either in the decision itself or through a "voluntary" change by the reporting institution.

It should also be noted that there are sanctions in the HCQIA for bad faith Peer Review. Hospitals lose their immunity for paying damages for improperly conducted or bad faith Peer Review. Some physicians have won such cases in court.

2. It seems reasonable to me that Peer Review be required to be essentially fair. Actions should not be overturned and reports voided simply because not every i was dotted or not every t was crossed. The system is, after all, designed ultimately to protect the public, not allow those who should be sanctioned to escape sanctions because of legal technicalities. Basic fairness should be the requirement. The law reflects this.

3. Providing an opportunity for truly independent Peer Review would be a great step forward. I generally endorse the suggestion for "permitting affected [physicians], at their cost, to opt for a hearing by a standing independent body of physicians in his or her own specialty." Depending on the nature of the offense, however, it may not be necessary to have physicians of the same specialty. Unacceptable behavior, as opposed to clinical competence, does not depend on specialty.

4. Establishing a threshold for reporting malpractice payments would be a major policy error. It would work against the interest of physicians because of the idea's unintended consequences. California had a system of reporting payments to the state which, essentially, did not require reporting to the state for possible public disclosure of payments under $30,000. These small payments, however, were reported to the NPDB. Almost 10 percent of all payments in California were for $29,999 – an amount almost never reported from any other state. It appeared that plaintiff's attorneys were holding out for $29,999 in cases which would have had lower payments or no payments at all by using the threat of a higher reportable payment if they took the case to *court I think the defense would offer $29,999 to ensure the case would "go away."*

5. I don't think it is in the public interest "to submit the malpractice claim for review to an independent body of physicians to determine whether the physician's conduct failed to meet the standard of care before reporting to the Data Bank." This would substitute a subjective standard (and one with a bit of fox guarding the hen house) for an objective one (payment made = report). Those who obtain reports know that some malpractice payments are made "for convenience," and many reports already contain a notation from the reporting insurer that they paid for convenience and that in their opinion the standard of care had been met. I would certainly not object to having this determination made by an "independent body" and noted in the report, but all payments should be reported. This ensures that those who receive the reports get full information and that they can evaluate individual payment reports to determine their significance or lack of significance.

6. This option already exists. Any institution can require "retraining and recertification of physicians by a university or specialty certification organization" instead of taking a reportable action. So long as clinical privileges are not negatively affected during the retraining and recertification process, the action is not reportable to the NPDB.

7. I tend to agree with the concept of "eliminat[ing] immunity for the sanctioning of physicians for "disagreeable" conduct that is based upon a legitimate, bona fide complaint or concern by the physician over the quality of care or other practices in a hospital, where the conduct of the physician is not shown to rise to the level of immediate, rather than theoretical risk of disruption and patient harm." The problem is in the implementation. Who is to judge whether there is a legitimate complaint or concern over quality of care or other practices and whether the risk to patients is immediate or only theoretical? Perhaps the independent Peer Review option suggested in # 3 is an answer.

8. "Requir[ing] a specific time frame for the Secretary of HH&S to act on objections by physicians to the propriety of filings with the National Practitioner Data Bank, so as to make the NPDB process meaningful and useful" sounds reasonable but is difficult, if not impossible, in practice. I cannot speak to the current situation, but while I was in charge of Secretarial Review, our goal was to close cases within a year if possible and to routinely do it much more quickly. We sometimes were unable to meet our goal, occasionally because of staffing shortages but more often because of lack of responsiveness by reporting institutions or by reported physicians to requests for additional information or because of the need to repeatedly request more information when only incomplete information was provided. I believe it is simply impractical to set a firm deadline for the conduct of reviews if the goal is to conduct them fairly based on complete information.

- Robert E. Oshel, Ph.D. RETIRED Associate Director for Research and Disputes, Division of Practitioner Data Banks, HRSA, US DHHS

DISCLAIMER: *The above comments represent my personal opinions and are not meant to represent either the current or previous positions of my pre-retirement employer, the U.S. Department of Health and Human Services*

APPENDIX

Healthcare Quality Improvement Act of 1986

P.L. 99–660, Approved November 14, 1986 (100 Stat. 3743)
Title IV-HealthCare Quality Improvement Act of 1986
* * * * * * *

TITLE IV—ENCOURAGING GOOD FAITH PROFESSIONAL REVIEW ACTIVITIES
SEC. 401.[42 U.S.C. 11101 note] SHORT TITLE.
This title may be cited as the "HealthCare Quality Improvement Act of 1986".
SEC. 402. [42 U.S.C. 11101] FINDINGS.
The Congress finds the following:

(1) The increasing occurrence of medical malpractice and the need to improve the quality of medical care have become nationwide problems that warrant greater efforts than those that can be undertaken by any individual State.

(2) There is a national need to restrict the ability of incompetent physicians to move from State to State without disclosure or discovery of the physician's previous damaging or incompetent performance.

(3) This nationwide problem can be remedied through effective professional Peer Review.

(4) The threat of private money damage liability under Federal laws, including treble damage liability under Federal antitrust law, unreasonably discourages physicians from participating in effective professional Peer Review.

(5) There is an overriding national need to provide incentive and protection for physicians engaging in effective professional Peer Review.
PART A—PROMOTION OF PROFESSIONAL REVIEW ACTIVITIES
SEC. 411.[42 U.S.C. 11111] PROFESSIONAL REVIEW.
(a) In General.—

(1) Limitation on damages for professional review actions.—If a professional review action (as defined in section 431(9)) of a professional review body meets all

146

the standards specified in section 412(a), except as provided in subsection (b)—

    (A) the professional review body,

    (B) any person acting as a member or staff to the body,

    (C) any person under a contract or other formal agreement with the body, and

    (D) any person who participates with or assists the body with respect to the action,

shall not be liable in damages under any law of the United States or of any State (or political subdivision thereof) with respect to the action. The preceding sentence shall not apply to damages under any law of the United States or any State relating to the civil rights of any person or persons, including the Civil Rights Act of 1964, 42 U.S.C. 2000e, et seq. and the Civil Rights Acts, 42 U.S.C. 1981, et seq. Nothing in this paragraph shall prevent the United States or any Attorney General of a State from bringing an action, including an action under section 4C of the Clayton Act, 15 U.S.C. 15C[219], where such an action is otherwise authorized.

    (2) Protection for those providing information to professional review bodies.— Notwithstanding any other provision of law, no person (whether as a witness or otherwise) providing information to a professional review body regarding the competence or professional conduct of a physician shall be held, by reason of having provided such information, to be liable in damages under any law of the United States or of any State (or political subdivision thereof) unless such information is false and the person providing it knew that such information was false.

(b) Exception.— If the Secretary has reason to believe that a healthcare entity has failed to report information in accordance with section 423(a), the Secretary shall conduct an investigation. If, after providing notice of noncompliance, an opportunity to correct the noncompliance, and an opportunity for a hearing, the Secretary determines that a healthcare entity has failed substantially to report information in accordance with section 423(a), the Secretary shall publish the name of the entity in the Federal Register. The protections of subsection (a)(1) shall not apply to an entity the name of which is published in the Federal Register under the previous sentence with respect to professional review actions of the entity commenced during the

3-year period beginning 30 days after the date of publication of the name.

(c) Treatment Under State Laws.—

(1) Professional review actions taken on or after October 14, 1989.— Except as provided in paragraph (2), subsection (a) shall apply to State laws in a State only for professional review actions commenced on or after October 14, 1989.

(2) Exceptions.—

(A) State early opt-in.— Subsection (a) shall apply to State laws in a State for actions commenced before October 14, 1989, if the State by legislation elects such treatment.

(B) Effective date of election.— An election under State law is not effective, for purposes of,[220] for actions commenced before the effective date of the State law, which may not be earlier than the date of the enactment of that law.

SEC. 412.[42 U.S.C. 11112] STANDARDS FOR PROFESSIONAL REVIEW ACTIONS.

(a) In General.— For purposes of the protection set forth in section 411(a), a professional review action must be taken —

(1) in the reasonable belief that the action was in the furtherance of quality healthcare,

(2) after a reasonable effort to obtain the facts of the matter,

(3) after adequate notice and hearing procedures are afforded to the physician involved or after such other procedures as are fair to the physician under the circumstances, and

(4) in the reasonable belief that the action was warranted by the facts known after such reasonable effort to obtain facts and after meeting the requirement of paragraph (3).

A professional review action shall be presumed to have met the preceding standards necessary for the protection set out in section 411(a) unless the presumption is rebutted by a preponderance of the evidence.

(b) Adequate Notice and Hearing.— A healthcare entity is deemed to have met the adequate notice and hearing requirement of subsection (a)(3) with respect to a physician if the following conditions are met (or are waived voluntarily by the physician):

(1) Notice of proposed action.— The physician has been given notice stating—

(A)(i) that a professional review action has been proposed to be taken against the physician,

(ii) reasons for the proposed action,

(B)(i) that the physician has the right to request a hearing on the proposed action,

(ii) any time limit (of not less than 30 days) within which to request such a hearing, and

(C) a summary of the rights in the hearing under paragraph (3).

(2) Notice of hearing.— If a hearing is requested on a timely basis under paragraph (1)(B), the physician involved must be given notice stating —

(A) the place, time, and date, of the hearing, which date shall not be less than 30 days after the date of the notice, and

(B) a list of the witnesses (if any) expected to testify at the hearing on behalf of the professional review body.

(3) Conduct of hearing and notice.— If a hearing is requested on a timely basis under paragraph (1)(B) —

(A) subject to subparagraph (B), the hearing shall be held (as determined by the healthcare entity) —

(i) before an arbitrator mutually acceptable to the physician and the healthcare entity,

(ii) before a hearing officer who is appointed by the entity and who is not in direct economic competition with the physician involved, or

(iii) before a panel of individuals who are appointed by the entity and are not in direct economic competition with the physician involved;

(B) the right to the hearing may be forfeited if the physician fails, without good cause, to appear;

(C) in the hearing the physician involved has the right —

(i) to representation by an attorney or other person of the physician's choice,

(ii) to have a record made of the proceedings, copies of which may be obtained by the physician upon payment of any reasonable charges associated with the preparation thereof,

(iii) to call, examine, and cross-examine witnesses,

(iv) to present evidence determined to be relevant by the hearing officer, regardless of its admissibility in a court of law, and

(v) to submit a written statement at the close of the hearing; and

(D) upon completion of the hearing, the physician involved has the right —

(i) to receive the written recommendation of the arbitrator, officer, or panel, including a statement of the basis for the recommendations, and

(ii) to receive a written decision of the healthcare entity, including a statement of the basis for the decision.

A professional review body's failure to meet the conditions described in this subsection shall not, in itself, constitute failure to meet the standards of subsection (a)(3).

(c) Adequate Procedures in Investigations or Health Emergencies.— For purposes of section 411(a), nothing in this section shall be construed as —

(1) requiring the procedures referred to in subsection (a)(3) —

(A) where there is no adverse professional review action taken, or

(B) in the case of a suspension or restriction of clinical privileges, for a period of not longer than 14 days, during which an investigation is being conducted to determine the need for a professional review action; or

(2) precluding an immediate suspension or restriction of clinical privileges, subject to subsequent notice and hearing or other adequate procedures, where the failure to take such an action may result in an imminent danger to the health of any individual.

SEC. 413. [42 U.S.C. 11113] PAYMENT OF REASONABLE ATTORNEYS' FEES AND COSTS IN DEFENSE OF SUIT.

In any suit brought against a defendant, to the extent that a defendant has met the standards set forth under section 412(a) and the defendant substantially prevails, the court shall, at the conclusion of the action, award to a substantially prevailing party defending against any such claim the cost of the suit attributable to such claim, including a reasonable attorney's fee, if the claim, or the claimant's conduct during the litigation of the claim, was frivolous, unreasonable, without foundation, or in bad faith. For the purposes of this section, a defendant shall not be considered to have substantially prevailed when the plaintiff obtains an award for damages or permanent injunctive or declaratory relief.

SEC. 414. [42 U.S.C. 11114] GUIDELINES OF THE SECRETARY.

The Secretary may establish, after notice and opportunity for comment, such voluntary guidelines as may assist the professional review bodies in meeting the standards described in section 412(a).

SEC. 415. [42 U.S.C. 11115] CONSTRUCTION.

(a) In General.— Except as specifically provided in this part, nothing in this part shall be construed as changing the liabilities or immunities under law or as preempting or overriding any State law which provides incentives, immunities, or protection for those engaged in a professional review action that is in addition to or greater than that provided by this part.

(b) Scope of Clinical Privileges.— Nothing in this part shall be construed as requiring healthcare entities to provide clinical privileges to any or all classes or types of physicians or other licensed healthcare practitioners.

(c) Treatment of Nurses and Other Practitioners.— Nothing in this part shall be construed as affecting, or modifying any provision of Federal or State law, with respect to activities of professional review bodies regarding nurses, other licensed healthcare practitioners, or other health professionals who are not physicians.

(d) Treatment of Patient Malpractice Claims.— Nothing in this title shall be construed as affecting in any manner the rights and remedies afforded patients under any provision of Federal or State law to seek redress for any harm or injury suffered as a result of negligent treatment or care by any physician, healthcare practitioner, or healthcare entity, or as limiting any defenses or immunities available to any physician, healthcare practitioner, or healthcare entity.

SEC. 416. [42 U.S.C. 11111 note] EFFECTIVE DATE.

This part shall apply to professional review actions commenced on or after the date of the enactment of this Act.

PART B—REPORTING OF INFORMATION

SEC. 421. [42 U.S.C. 11131] REQUIRING REPORTS ON MEDICAL MALPRACTICE PAYMENTS.

(a) In General.— Each entity (including an insurance company) which makes payment under a policy of insurance, self-insurance, or otherwise in settlement (or partial settlement) of, or in satisfaction of a judgment in, a medical malpractice action or claim shall report, in accordance with section 424, information respecting the payment and circumstances thereof.

(b) Information To Be Reported — The information to be reported under subsection (a) includes —

(1) the name of any physician or licensed healthcare practitioner for whose benefit the payment is made,

(2) the amount of the payment,

(3) the name (if known) of any hospital with which the physician or practitioner is affiliated or associated,

(4) a description of the acts or omissions and injuries or illnesses upon which the action or claim was based, and

(5) such other information as the Secretary determines is required for appropriate interpretation of information reported under this section.

(c) Sanctions for Failure to Report. — Any entity that fails to report information on a payment required to be reported under this section shall be subject to a civil money penalty of not more than $10,000 for each such payment involved. Such penalty shall be imposed and collected in the same manner as civil money penalties under subsection (a) of section 1128A of the Social Security Act are imposed and collected under that section.

(d) Report on Treatment of Small Payments. — The Secretary shall study and report to Congress, not later than two years after the date of the enactment of this Act, on whether information respecting small payments should continue to be required to be reported under subsection (a) and whether information respecting all claims made concerning a medical malpractice action should be required to be reported under such subsection.

SEC. 422. [42 U.S.C. 11132] REPORTING OF SANCTIONS TAKEN BY BOARDS OF MEDICAL EXAMINERS.

(a) In General. —

(1) Actions subject to reporting. — Each Board of Medical Examiners —

(A) which revokes or suspends (or otherwise restricts) a physician's license or censures, reprimands, or places on probation a physician, for reasons relating to the physician's professional competence or professional conduct, or

(B) to which a physician's license is surrendered, shall report, in accordance with section 424, the information described in paragraph (2).

(2) Information to be reported.—The information to be reported under paragraph (1) is—

(A) the name of the physician involved,

(B) a description of the acts or omissions or other reasons (if known) for the revocation, suspension, or surrender of license, and

(C) such other information respecting the circumstances of the action or surrender as the Secretary deems appropriate.

(b) Failure to Report. — If, after notice of noncompliance and providing opportunity to correct noncompliance, the Secretary determines that a Board of Medical Examiners has failed to report information in accordance with subsection (a), the Secretary shall designate another qualified entity for the reporting of information under section 423.

SEC. 423. [42 U.S.C. 11133] REPORTING OF CERTAIN PROFESSIONAL REVIEW ACTIONS TAKEN BY HEALTHCARE ENTITIES.

(a) Reporting by HealthCare Entities. —

(1) On physicians. — Each healthcare entity which —

(A) takes a professional review action that adversely affects the clinical privileges of a physician for a period longer than 30 days;

(B) accepts the surrender of clinical privileges of a physician —

(i) while the physician is under an investigation by the entity relating to possible incompetence or improper professional conduct, or

(ii) in return for not conducting such an investigation or proceeding; or

(C) in the case of such an entity which is a professional society, takes a professional review action which adversely affects the membership of a physician in the society,shall report to the Board of Medical Examiners, in accordance with section 424(a), the information described in paragraph (3).

(2) Permissive reporting on other licensed healthcare practitioners. — A healthcare entity may report to the Board of Medical Examiners, in accordance with section 424(a), the information described in paragraph (3) in the case of a licensed healthcare practitioner who is not a physician, if the entity would be required to report such information under paragraph (1) with respect to the practitioner if the practitioner were a physician.

(3) Information to be reported. — The information to be reported under this subsection is —

(A) the name of the physician or practitioner involved,

(B) a description of the acts or omissions or other reasons for the action or, if known, for the surrender, and

(C) such other information respecting the circumstances of the action or surrender as the Secretary deems appropriate.

(b) Reporting by Board of Medical Examiners. — Each Board of Medical Examiners shall report, in accordance with section 424, the information reported to it under subsection (a) and known instances of a healthcare entity's failure to report information under subsection (a)(1).

(c) Sanctions. —

(1) Healthcare entities. — A healthcare entity that fails substantially to meet the requirement of subsection (a)(1) shall lose the protections of section 411(a)(1) if the

Secretary publishes the name of the entity under section 411(b).

(2) Board of medical examiners. — If, after notice of noncompliance and providing an opportunity to correct noncompliance, the Secretary determines that a Board of Medical Examiners has failed to report information in accordance with subsection (b), the Secretary shall designate another qualified entity for the reporting of information under subsection (b).

(d) References to Board of Medical Examiners. — Any reference in this part to a Board of Medical Examiners includes, in the case of a Board in a State that fails to meet the reporting requirements of section 422(a) or subsection (b), a reference to such other qualified entity as the Secretary designates.

SEC. 424. [42 U.S.C. 11134] FORM OF REPORTING.

(a) Timing and Form. — The information required to be reported under sections 421, 422(a), and 423 shall be reported regularly (but not less often than monthly) and in such form and manner as the Secretary prescribes. Such information shall first be required to be reported on a date (not later than one year after the date of the enactment of this Act) specified by the Secretary.

(b) To Whom Reported. — The information required to be reported under sections 421, 422(a), and 423(b) shall be reported to the Secretary, or, in the Secretary's discretion, to an appropriate private or public agency which has made suitable arrangements with the Secretary with respect to receipt, storage, protection of confidentiality, and dissemination of the information under this part.

(c) Reporting to State Licensing Boards. —

(1) Malpractice payments. — Information required to be reported under section 421 shall also be reported to the appropriate State licensing board (or boards) in the State in which the medical malpractice claim arose.

(2) Reporting to other licensing boards. — Information required to be reported under section 423(b) shall also be reported to the appropriate State licensing board in the State in which the healthcare entity is located if it is not otherwise reported to such board under subsection (b).

SEC. 425. [42 U.S.C. 11135] DUTY OF HOSPITALS TO OBTAIN INFORMATION.

(a) In General. — It is the duty of each hospital to request from the Secretary (or the agency designated under section 424(b)), on and after the date information is first required to be reported under section 424(a))[221] —

    (1) at the time a physician or licensed healthcare practitioner applies to be on the medical staff (courtesy or otherwise) of, or for clinical privileges at, the hospital, information reported under this part concerning the physician or practitioner, and

    (2) once every 2 years information reported under this part concerning any physician or such practitioner who is on the medical staff (courtesy or otherwise) of, or has been granted clinical privileges at, the hospital.

A hospital may request such information at other times.

(b) Failure to Obtain Information. — With respect to a medical malpractice action, a hospital which does not request information respecting a physician or practitioner as required under subsection (a) is presumed to have knowledge of any information reported under this part to the Secretary with respect to the physician or practitioner.

(c) Reliance on Information Provided. — Each hospital may rely upon information provided to the hospital under this title and shall not be held liable for such reliance in the absence of the hospital's knowledge that the information provided was false.

SEC. 426. [42 U.S.C. 11136] DISCLOSURE AND CORRECTION OF INFORMATION.

With respect to the information reported to the Secretary (or the agency designated under section 424(b)) under this part respecting a physician or other licensed healthcare practitioner, the Secretary shall, by regulation, provide for—

    (1) disclosure of the information, upon request, to the physician or practitioner, and

    (2) procedures in the case of disputed accuracy of the information.

SEC. 427. [42 U.S.C. 11137] MISCELLANEOUS PROVISIONS.

(a) Providing Licensing Boards and Other HealthCare Entities With Access to Information. — The Secretary (or the agency designated under section 424(b)) shall, upon request, provide information reported under this part with respect to a physician or other licensed healthcare practitioner to State licensing boards, to hospitals, and to other healthcare entities (including health maintenance organizations) that have entered (or may be entering) into an employment or affiliation relationship with the physician or practitioner or to which the physician or practitioner has applied for clinical privileges or appointment to the medical staff.

(b) Confidentiality of Information. —

(1) In general. — Information reported under this part is considered confidential and shall not be disclosed (other than to the physician or practitioner involved) except with respect to professional review activity, as necessary to carry out subsections (b) and (c) of section 425 (as specified in regulations by the Secretary), or in accordance with regulations of the Secretary promulgated pursuant to subsection (a). Nothing in this subsection shall prevent the disclosure of such information by a party which is otherwise authorized, under applicable State law, to make such disclosure. Information reported under this part that is in a form that does not permit the identification of any particular healthcare entity, physician, other healthcare practitioner, or patient shall not be considered confidential. The Secretary (or the agency designated under section 424(b)), on application by any person, shall prepare such information in such form and shall disclose such information in such form.

(2) Penalty for violations. — Any person who violates paragraph (1) shall be subject to a civil money penalty of not more than $10,000 for each such violation involved. Such penalty shall be imposed and collected in the same manner as civil money penalties under subsection (a) of section 1128A of the Social Security Act are imposed and collected under that section.

(3) Use of information. — Subject to paragraph (1), information provided under section 425 and subsection (a) is intended to be used solely with respect to activities in the furtherance of the quality of healthcare.

(4) Fees. — The Secretary may establish or approve reasonable fees for the disclosure of information under this section or section 426. The amount of such a fee may not exceed the costs of processing the requests for disclosure and of providing such information. Such fees shall be available to the Secretary (or, in the Secretary's discretion, to the agency designated under section 424(b)) to cover such costs.

(c) Relief From Liability for Reporting. — No person or entity (including the agency designated under section 424(b)) shall be held liable in any civil action with respect to any report made under this part (including information provided under subsection (a) without knowledge of the falsity of the information contained in the report.

(d) Interpretation of Information. — In interpreting information reported under this part, a payment in settlement of a medical malpractice action or claim shall not be construed as creating a presumption that medical malpractice has occurred.

PART C — DEFINITIONS AND REPORTS

SEC. 431. [42 U.S.C. 11151] DEFINITIONS.

In this title:

(1) The term "adversely affecting" includes reducing, restricting, suspending, revoking, denying, or failing to renew clinical privileges or membership in a healthcare entity.

(2) The term "Board of Medical Examiners" includes a body comparable to such a Board (as determined by the State) with responsibility for the licensing of physicians and also includes a subdivision of such a Board or body.

(3) The term "clinical privileges" includes privileges, membership on the medical staff, and the other circumstances pertaining to the furnishing of medical care under which a physician or other licensed healthcare practitioner is permitted to furnish such care by a healthcare entity.

(4)(A) The term "healthcare entity" means —

(i) a hospital that is licensed to provide healthcare services by the State in which it is located,

(ii) an entity (including a health maintenance organization or group medical practice) that provides healthcare services and that follows a formal Peer Review process for the purpose of furthering quality healthcare (as determined under regulations of the Secretary), and

(iii) subject to subparagraph (B), a professional society (or committee thereof) of physicians or other licensed healthcare practitioners that follows a formal Peer

Review process for the purpose of furthering quality healthcare (as determined under regulations of the Secretary).

(B) The term "healthcare entity" does not include a professional society (or committee thereof) if, within the previous 5 years, the society has been found by the Federal Trade Commission or any court to have engaged in any anticompetitive practice which had the effect of restricting the practice of licensed healthcare practitioners.

(5) The term "hospital" means an entity described in paragraphs (1) and (7) of section 1861(e) of the Social Security Act.

(6) The terms "licensed healthcare practitioner" and "practitioner" mean, with respect to a State, an individual (other than a physician) who is licensed or otherwise authorized by the State to provide healthcare services.

(7) The term "medical malpractice action or claim" means a written claim or demand for payment based on a healthcare provider's furnishing (or failure to furnish) healthcare services, and includes the filing of a cause of action, based on the law of tort, brought in any court of any State or the United States seeking monetary damages.

(8) The term "physician" means a doctor of medicine or osteopathy or a doctor of dental surgery or medical dentistry legally authorized to practice medicine and surgery or dentistry by a State (or any individual who, without authority holds himself or herself out to be so authorized).

(9) The term "professional review action" means an action or recommendation of a professional review body which is taken or made in the conduct of professional review activity, which is based on the competence or professional conduct of an individual physician (which conduct affects or could affect adversely the health or welfare of a patient or patients), and which affects (or may affect) adversely the clinical privileges, or membership in a professional society, of the physician. Such term includes a formal decision of a professional review body not to take an action or make a

recommendation described in the previous sentence and also includes professional review activities relating to a professional review action. In this title, an action is not considered to be based on the competence or professional conduct of a physician if the action is primarily based on —

(A) the physician's association, or lack of association, with a professional society or association,

(B) the physician's fees or the physician's advertising or engaging in other competitive acts intended to solicit or retain business,

(C) the physician's participation in prepaid group health plans, salaried employment, or any other manner of delivering health services whether on a fee-for-service or other basis,

(D) a physician's association with, supervision of, delegation of authority to, support for, training of, or participation in a private group practice with, a member or members of a particular class of healthcare practitioner or professional, or

(E) any other matter than does not relate to the competence or professional conduct of a physician.

(10) The term "professional review activity" means an activity of a healthcare entity with respect to an individual physician —

(A) to determine whether the physician may have clinical privileges with respect to, or membership in, the entity,

(B) to determine the scope or conditions of such privileges or membership, or

(C) to change or modify such privileges or membership.

(11) The term "professional review body" means a healthcare entity and the governing body or any committee of a healthcare entity which conducts professional review activity, and includes any committee of the medical staff of such an entity when assisting the governing body in a professional review activity.

(12) The term "Secretary" means the Secretary of Health and Human Services.

(13) The term "State" means the 50 States, the District of Columbia, Puerto Rico, the Virgin Islands, Guam, American Samoa, and the Northern Mariana Islands.

(14) The term "State licensing board" means, with respect to a physician or healthcare provider in a State, the agency of the State, which is primarily responsible for the licensing of the physician or provider to furnish healthcare services.

SEC. 432. [42 U.S.C. 11152] REPORTS AND MEMORANDA OF UNDERSTANDING.

(a) Annual Reports to Congress. — The Secretary shall report to Congress, annually during the three years after the date of the enactment of this Act, on the implementation of this title.

(b) Memoranda of Understanding. — The Secretary of Health and Human Services shall seek to enter into memoranda of understanding with the Secretary of Defense and the Administrator of Veterans' Affairs to apply the provisions of part B of this title to hospitals and other facilities and healthcare providers under the jurisdiction of the Secretary or Administrator, respectively. The Secretary shall report to Congress, not later than two years after the date of the enactment of this Act, on any such memoranda and on the cooperation among such officials in establishing such memoranda.

(c) Memorandum of Understanding with Drug Enforcement Administration. — The Secretary of Health and Human Services shall seek to enter into a memorandum of understanding with the Administrator of Drug Enforcement relating to providing for the reporting by the Administrator to the Secretary of information respecting physicians and other practitioners whose registration to dispense controlled substances has been suspended or revoked under section 304 of the Controlled Substances Act. The Secretary shall report to Congress, not later than two years after the date of the enactment of this Act, on any such memorandum and on the cooperation between the Secretary and the Administrator in establishing such a memorandum.

*　*　*　*　*　*　*

[Internal References. — SSAct §1921(b) cites the HealthCare Quality Improvement Act of 1986. SSAct Title XVIII heading has a footnote referring to P.L. 99-660.]

[219] As in original; should be "15 U.S.C. 15c".
[220] As in original.
[221] As in original; closing parenthesis should be deleted.

ABOUT THE AUTHOR

GREGORY R. PICHÉ

Overview:

Opened a virtual healthcare practice firm, Singularity Health Law, PLLC on January 1, 2011. Practiced healthcare law at Holland & Hart and a tributary firm since 1973. Served as leader of the firm's healthcare practice group for more than 20 years. Holland & Hart is a 450-attorney law firm with 15 offices across the Mountain West.

Managed a wide variety of healthcare, legal representation in both counseling and litigation for and on behalf of hospitals, physicians, physician networks, limited license providers, nursing homes, durable medical equipment providers, home health agencies, healthcare service providers and managed care companies.

Representation includes compliance counseling for HIPAA, Stark law, Anti-kickback Statute, CMP and "fraud and abuse" defense, healthcare criminal defense, joint ventures, anti-trust, professional license disputes, provider fair hearings, state and federal administrative appeals, provider-hospital disputes, business torts, management services contracts, employment contracts and managed care service contracts.

Introduced healthcare law log that is a leading source of legal insight in the profession as well as being the first legal 'blawg' by an Amlaw 200 firm. Known as a high energy and innovative lawyer who cares deeply for his clients and colleagues. Frequent speaker, author and expert on legal issues facing healthcare providers.

Experience:

- Founder of Holland & Hart healthcare practice representing hospitals, professionals, and healthcare related firms in counseling, business transactions, regulatory compliance and litigation.

- Developed multi-state, regional practice in healthcare law.

- Obtained compliance from the U.S. Department of Labor for healthcare benefits due to cancer ridden former nuclear energy workers through class action lawsuit.

- Overturned exclusion of healthcare agency banned from participation in Medicare by Centers for Medicare and Medicaid Services.

- Developed antitrust, HIPAA and fraud and abuse compliance programs for hospital systems and hospitals in various states.

- Served as outside general counsel for large Catholic hospital system.

- Served as special counsel to board of trustees of a university hospital.

- Restored and exonerated a fired university medical school professor and world-renowned clinician.

- Nominated twice to the Colorado Court of Appeals by the Colorado Supreme Court nominating committee.

- Chaired Litigation Section of the Colorado Bar Association. Developed innovative, award winning, healthcare law blog with large internet presence and international following (see blog web address below).

- Served on U.S. District Court Peer Review committee and Colorado Supreme Court Civil Rules Committee.

- Serving as only lawyer member of the University Of Colorado School Of Business Program in Hospital and Healthcare Administration.

- Active in dispute and conflict resolution reform in state and federal practice.

- Frequent speaker at national and regional healthcare events and programs on topics such as healthcare reform, clinical integration, the uses of brain scans in litigation and the legal status of TPA in the treatment of ischemic stroke victims.

- As Chairman of the Colorado Bar Association's Jury Reform Committee, introduced the "one day/one trial" jury service system to Colorado and co-authored the jury orientation audiovisual program shown daily in state courts throughout Colorado. The "one day/one trial" system in Colorado substantially reduced jury service time.

Publications

Blog author of approximately 500 articles on healthcare law and issues published on the Internet. (2003-2011). Singularity Health Law Blog, (www.singularitylaw.net)

Chapter author, Successful Strategies for Dealing with Government Agencies in HealthCare Law: Leading Lawyers on interacting With State and Federal Agencies, Understanding Potential Legal Issues, and Navigating an Ever-Changing Regulatory Environment. Aspatore Books (June, 2007) ISBN: 9781596227958.

Faculty chairman, co-author and editor of The Federal Rules of Evidence Self Assessment Program, and of an ongoing experiment in participatory continuing legal education cosponsored by Continuing Legal Education in Colorado, Inc. and Professional Evaluation and Publication Services, Inc. of Philadelphia, Pennsylvania.

Publications include "New Advocacy in Mental Health Representation," The Colorado Lawyer, 1977; "Medical Confidentiality - An Overview," Rocky Mountain Medical Journal, July/August 1979; "Dodging the Bullet - Avoiding Conspiracy Claims in Professional Staff Disputes," Hospitals and Health Services Administration, Winter, 1988; "Confidentiality of Medical Records," Lorman Business Center, Inc., 1988.

Pro Bono:

Represented three convicted death row inmates in Texas and Oklahoma in appellate and post-conviction hearings, where fair process had been denied.

Challenged constitutionality of state exclusion of legal aliens from state Medicaid coverage and obtained stay of exclusion for seriously ill patients.

Education

Michigan State University (J.D.)
University of Michigan (B.A., Economics)

Admissions and Awards

Admitted to practice in Colorado and Michigan
Martindale Ranking: A/V Rated
Colorado Superlawyers

Professional Affiliations

Member, American Health Lawyer's Association
Member, Medical Group Management Association
Member, Healthcare Financial Management Association
Member, Criminal Justice Act Panel
Past Member, Colorado Bar Association Board of Governors
Past Trustee, Pikes Peak Legal Services Corporation
Past Member, Colorado Supreme Court Civil Rules Committee
Past Chairman, Litigation Section of the Colorado Bar Association

Community Service
Past President, Museum of Contemporary Art /Denver

Board Member, Museo de las Americas
Member, University of Colorado at Denver, School of
  Hospital and Health Administration Advisory Board

CONTACT
GREGORY R. PICHÉ

Singularity Legal, PLLC
3144 Newton St.
Denver, CO 80211

Telephone: 303- 668-4240

greg@singularitylaw.net

website: www.gregorypiche.com

blog: singularitylaw.net

www.ingramcontent.com/pod-product-compliance
Lightning Source LLC
Chambersburg PA
CBHW051506170526
45166CB00001B/405